R. D. & Patricia P.

Monitors, Tegus, and Related Lizards

Everything about Selection, Care, Nutrition,
Diseases, Breeding, and Behavior

With 58 Color Photographs

Illustrations by Laura Barghusen

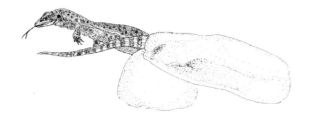

BARRON'S

Acknowledgments

To Bill Love and Rob MacInnes of Glades, Herp, Inc. (Ft. Myers, Florida), we extend thanks for the photographic opportunities. They and their breeding farm manager, Chuck Hurt, unhesitatingly provided us with information regarding their breeding programs for Merten's and "Ionides" monitors and red tegus. Bert and Hester Langerwerf of Agama International (Montevallo, Alabama) shared their thoughts on breeding black and white tegus. Their continued success with this impressive lizard species is to be lauded. We are also grateful to longtime "varaniphile" and researcher, Robert G. Sprackland, who provided us with discussion and research papers.

Finally, a special note of appreciation to Fredric L. Frye, DVM, for his critical evaluation and pertinent contributions to our manuscript.

All inquiries should be addressed to:
Barron's Educational Series, Inc.
250 Wireless Boulevard
Hauppauge, NY 11788

International Standard Book No. 0-8120-9696-7

Library of Congress Catalog Card No. 96-19488

Library of Congress Cataloging-in-Publication Data

Bartlett, Richard D., 1938–
    Monitors, tegus, and related lizards / by
R. D. & Patricia P. Bartlett ; illustrations by Laura
Barghusen.
        p.   cm. — (A Complete pet owner's manual)
    Includes bibliographical references (p. 99) and
index.
    ISBN 0-8120-9696-7
    1. Monitor lizards as pets. 2. Teiidae. 3. Lizards
as pets. I. Bartlett, Patricia Pope, 1949– . II. Title.
III. Series.
SF459.L5B37   1996
639.3′95—dc20   96-19488
                       CIP

Printed in Hong Kong

987654

About the Authors

R. D. Bartlett is a herpetologist who has authored more than 425 articles and three books, and coauthored an additional eight books. He lectures extensively and has participated in field studies across North and Latin America. In 1970 he began the Reptilian Breeding and Research Institute, a private facility. Since its inception, more than 200 species of reptiles and amphibians have been bred at RBRI, some for the first time in the United States under captive conditions. Successes at the RBRI include several endangered species.

Bartlett is a member of numerous herpetological and conservation organizations, a cohost on an "on-line" reptile and amphibian forum, and a contributing editor of *Reptiles* Magazine.

Patricia Bartlett is a biologist and historian who has authored five books and coauthored eight books. A museum administrator for the last fifteen years, she has worked in both history and science museums.

Photo Credits

Zig Leszczynski: inside back cover, pages 15, 18, 22, 36, 50, 53 bottom, 56 bottom, 62, 63, 67, 79, 86, and 90; Karl H. Switak: pages 7, 11, 26, 49, 52, 82, and 83 top; all other photographs by R. D. Bartlett.

Additional illustrations supplied by Michele Earle-Bridges and Tom Kerr.

Cover Photos

Front cover; Nile monitor, *Varanus n. niloticus;* inside front cover: white-throated monitor, *Varanus a. albigularis;* inside back cover: emerald monitor, *Varanus prasinus;* back cover: white-throated monitor, *Varanus a. albigularis*

Important Notes

Caution should be exercised before using any of the electrical equipment described in this book.

While handling monitors, tegus and other lizards you may occasionally receive bites or scratches. If your skin is broken, see your physician immediately.

Some terrarium plants may be harmful to the skin or mucous membranes of human beings. If you notice any signs of irritation, wash the area thoroughly. See your physician if the condition persists.

Monitors, tegus and other lizards may transmit certain infections to humans. Always wash your hands carefully after handling your specimens. Always supervise children who wish to observe your lizards.

Contents

Preface

This book is about monitors and tegus, lizards of two different families, some of which grow to a considerable size. Several species of these lizards are commonly available in the pet trade, and their care requirements are much alike. The first chapters of this book cover equivalent care requirements of these lizards. The second part of the book discusses the monitors (also referred to as varanids, for their family Varanidae) and the third, the tegus (also called teiids for their family Teiidae) and their immediate relatives.

When we first began keeping monitors and tegus, there weren't a great number of species available. Eight or ten monitors and perhaps two or three tegus—all wild-caught—were all that one expected to encounter. Although the species have changed somewhat, today there remain just six to ten monitors seen with any regularity in the American pet trade, and the number of commonly seen teiid species has dropped to one, and, sadly, most specimens remain wild-caught.

In those early days, information on the field of reptile husbandry was limited to a list of a dozen 1930s to 1960s books that mentioned diet or perhaps habitat details just in passing. The idea of going out in the field just to look at reptiles was greeted largely with snorts of disbelief. Neither herpetology nor herpetoculture were "mainstream."

Today things have changed, but from the monitor's and tegu's vantage points, not necessarily for the better.

Suitable habitats have dwindled, lizard-skin leather goods are fashionable, the keeping of reptiles has become an accepted and interactive hobby, and the pressures on the existing monitor and tegu populations elevate daily. Our knowledge of monitor and tegu husbandry and breeding lags far behind that for many other lizards.

But we're improving. Some of the once uncommonly seen monitors and tegus have become the focus for captive-breeding, and hobbyists are even trying to breed some of the more commonly imported and inexpensive species. Bookshelves groan under the weight of books and magazines, and enthusiasts exchange husbandry data worldwide on-line and via E-mail. Concepts such as "conservation" and "ethics" are becoming more than mere words, and reptile-oriented ecotourism companies are guiding hobbyists on monitor and tegu photographing excursions across the world.

The dedicated monitor and tegu watchers and keepers, whether hobbyists or professionals, deserve the thanks and credit for these changes. Their work in observing, breeding, and sharing information about these lizards has made it possible for all of us to learn about them.

No matter which type of lizard appeals to you more, we urge you to keep notes on your animal and its behavior and to share your findings with others. As the natural habitats for these animals decrease, our need for responsible care in all cases increases.

4

Understanding Your Monitor or Tegu

The long-bodied, agile monitors and tegus, respectively Old World and New World lizards, display a great deal of morphological variety. They range in size from 8 inches (20 cm) to 10 feet (3 m), and in temperament from placid to openly hostile. These denizens of deserts, forests, and savannas are active hunters and scavengers, and their caging and feeding must reflect their specialized needs.

The young of a great many monitors—even some that are predominantly terrestrial when adult—are highly arboreal, which keeps many juveniles out of the casual reach of predatory larger specimens. When planning caging, this propensity of the young to climb needs to be considered. Even the adults of many large monitor species ("large" means adult length of 4 feet [1.3 m] or more) are agile climbers, readily taking to a tree or other vertical rise to pursue prey or escape danger. Teiids are not quite the climbers that the younger monitors are, but if warm they are still fast-moving lizards that can dart through a cage opening faster than the keeper can react.

The degree of tameness that you can expect from your monitor or tegu will depend on the species, as well as the amount of gentle handling to which the lizard is subjected. Some species seem better able than others to adjust to the rigors of captive life. The sharp teeth and claws and, to a lesser degree, the whipping tail of a monitor or tegu of even moderate size can prove adequately discomfiting to dissuade friendly overtures by all but the most dedicated keepers. To augment these defensive tactics, frightened monitors will also void their intestinal contents on a careless handler, in itself a discouraging habit.

Choosing a Monitor or Tegu

Caring for one or more monitor or tegu lizards is an ongoing task, and choosing the wrong species, for whatever reason, can greatly reduce the enjoyment you hoped to feel when you chose your scaly pet.

Unless you are able and willing to provide a nearly room-sized cage for your monitor, you really don't want a Nile or Asian water monitor, and you may not really want a savanna monitor, only slightly smaller and with just slightly smaller caging needs.

Even if you *are* willing to devote a room-sized cage to a Nile monitor, will you be able to provide and keep clean the bathtub-sized water receptacle that these semiaquatic saurians should have?

It is not always easy to get rid of big monitors. This is true even if they're tame, and especially true if they are a little less than wholly trustworthy.

Cost, besides space and ready availability, is a factor to most hobbyists. Once you decide you're not going to purchase one of the readily available (generally large) and inexpensive species (baby Niles and savannas sell for about $50 dollars), you begin to talk about spending big money for

The young of many monitors (and the adults of some) are highly arboreal. Pictured is an emerald tree monitor, Varanus prasinus.

sunken. The long tongue should be protruded and flicked as the lizard investigates its quarters or a disturbance. The body weight should be average to heavy, not thin with obviously protruding ribs and pelvis. The skin should not be hanging in loose folds. Whenever possible, watch the animal feed. If kept properly, a healthy monitor that is acclimating well should willingly feed within a day or two after it has been received. If it does not feed, we suggest that you not buy it.

Highly aggressive monitors or tegus or those that are otherwise severely stressed should also be avoided. These will often not acclimate to a point where they can be handled and may even refuse to feed in captivity.

Note: Wild-collected adult monitors and tegus are poor candidates for a satisfying lizard-owner relationship. Avoid these if it is an easily handled pet you are interested in.

While baby and subadult monitors and tegus can be housed communally, adults tend to live a solitary existence. Males stake out their territories and defend those territories vigorously against incursions by other males of their species. Females are usually much less territorial.

Two maturing male monitors or tegus that have been housed together since babyhood are very likely to become incompatible with age. Be prepared to separate them when agonistic behavior starts.

Captive-Raised versus Wild-Collected

Until very recently, all monitors, tegus, and relatives offered for sale in the pet marketplaces of the world were wild-collected. European hobbyists were probably the first to develop accurate methods of sexing and breeding many species of the enigmatic and coveted types of monitors, but tegus are not yet as popular with breeders.

your monitors. For example, mangrove monitors now sell for about $150, Dumeril's for $200, rough-necked for $300, Australian ridge-tails for $700 and Storr's for $1,000. It may take a considerable cash outlay to purchase a type best suited for your conditions.

The tegus are the same way. The very commonly imported Amazonian black and yellow tegu, a species that can be difficult to tame, often sells in the pet marketplace for as little as $30 each. However, the more coveted red and black and white tegus usually bring somewhat more than $250 each. The more unusual types, such as the big red-headed green caiman lizard, may sell for several times the price of a black and white, and this type of caiman lizard can be very difficult to acclimate.

Health, of course, should also be a major deciding factor in the acquisition of any monitor or tegu. The animal you choose should *look* good. The eyes should be clear, bright, inquisitive, and rounded, not encrusted, dull, or

Threat or defense postures include a distended throat and tensed body. This is an Australian argus monitor (V. p. panoptes) *in its habitat.*

Small numbers of a few monitor species and two species of tegus are now being bred by American herpeto-culturists, but the Europeans continue to remain far in the lead with the monitor species.

Captive-breeding programs in America are now producing species as diverse as the beautiful Australian spiny-tailed monitor, as well as a few specimens of the long-endangered Bengal monitor. The fact that these are both expensive species that are not easily imported from the wild makes breeding them monetarily worthwhile. To purchase or barter a Bengal or any other endangered monitor species in United States interstate commerce requires a Federal permit.

On the other hand, both Nile and savanna monitors are imported from the wild so cheaply that breeders simply could not compete in price. Thus, no serious captive-breeding programs are yet in place for these popular species.

We strongly recommend that, when available, captive-bred and hatched monitors and tegus be purchased by enthusiasts. This will ultimately not only reduce collecting pressures, but will rather assure you of acquiring acclimated, nonstressed, nearly (or entirely) parasite-free specimens.

Although the cost of captive-bred specimens may be slightly greater than that of imported specimens, the difference will be money well spent.

In today's increasingly conservation-oriented society, purchasing captive-bred and hatched specimens is the responsible thing to do.

Caging

A hobbyist's purchase of a monitor, especially of a large species, is all too often wrongly on impulse. It is hard for even those who have seen and handled adult monitors to visualize the adult size from that 8-inch (20 cm) baby savanna, or the 10-inch (25 cm) baby Nile monitor in the 10-gallon (38 L) tank in the pet store. An increase of a hundred times (or more!) in overall bulk is not only possible—it is *probable.* Coupled with the increase in size is the real possibility that the disposition of your adult monitor may not be entirely benign.

But it's time now to discuss caging. It stands to reason that small monitor and tegu species are easier to house at all stages of their life than large species. Equally obvious is the fact that if you choose a medium-to-large monitor species, arid-land and savanna dwellers are more easily housed than persistently aquatic species. You simply don't need to provide and continually clean a large volume of water for the arid-land forms (see also pages 21 to 24 and individual species accounts).

Cage Size

A monitor of 6 feet (2 m) or more in length should be provided with an enclosure at least the size of a room, furnished with tree trunks and inclined limbs, elevated shelves, access to natural sunlight or a bank of UV (ultraviolet)-producing lights, a hot-spot basking area, areas of seclusion, and an adequate supply of clean water.

Indeed, many keepers of large monitors actually donate a spare room to their charge.

No matter the size of the lizards, monitors and tegus that you hope to breed should be provided with proportionately more room than otherwise, and of course the cages for groups of lizards should be larger yet than for only a single specimen.

Indoor cages can be custom-made or adapted from suitably sized aquaria. No matter which, cages must close tightly and lock. Sides must be of welded wire rather than screen, which can be torn by the sharp claws of only moderately large monitors and tegus.

If you choose to make your own wood-framed cage, it is a small matter to hinge and secure a top. If the top is separate from the cage, use clamps or place a brick atop each end to discourage unauthorized "wanderings." The precaution may not be attractive, but it is functional.

As your lizard grows, it will require correspondingly more space. Eventually, a large custom-built cage (which

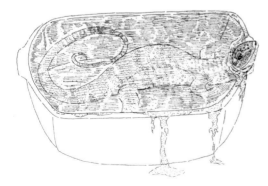

Mangrove monitor lying in water dish.

will quickly become the focal point of a room)—or the room itself—will be required to house the lizard.

Don't let the term "custom-made" scare you. Anyone with even a moderate skill in carpentry can make a suitable cage in an evening. If you know how to hammer, staple and use a saw, you can make a cage.

A simple cage begins with a wooden framework. Welded wire mesh is stapled to the outside of the framework. The bottom can be a piece of waterproof plywood (¾ inch [.9 cm] is best, but ½ inch [1.3 cm] will do). The bottom can be wire mesh if the cage sits atop a bed of newspaper. During the colder months, to facilitate warming the cage, you may have to staple pliofilm to the outside; a minimum of 4 mil thickness is suggested. The supporting braces will need to be at least 2 × 2s (5 × 5 cm) or better, 2 × 4s (5 × 10 cm), and the wire mesh 2 × ½ inch (5 × 1.3 cm). A smaller mesh is apt to catch the toenails of the monitors and tegus and could cause injury to the toes. If a smooth welded mesh is used, it will help prevent the lizard from abrading its nose if it tries to escape. The braces can be nailed or screwed together and the mesh stapled on with a staple gun. Be sure the door is large enough for you to reach to the bottom of the cage to clean it, or add another door at the bottom of the cage for this purpose.

If you prefer a heavier cage, you can build one from plywood sheeting with wood-framed glass doors. The plywood cage will require sizable screened ventilation panels on each end. If wire is used in the ventilation panels, make certain it is welded and a large enough mesh to avoid injury.

For moderate to large (2.5 to 4 feet (.8–1.2 m), plus) arboreal monitors, we provide a vertically oriented cage, 6 feet (2 m) in length, and just narrow and low enough to be moved through

Room-sized caging for monitor.

a doorway—approximately 30 inches (75 cm) wide × 6 feet (2 m) high. This allows the cage to be moved outside in good weather and brought inside in bad weather. To facilitate this move, the cage is set on a series of casters (wheels). If your cage is glass, set it on a plywood platform that is on casters. The bigger the casters, the better.

If your monitor or tegu is out of its cage roaming about your room or home much of the time, a somewhat smaller cage would be acceptable. In all cases, your lizard should be able to stretch out its full length to bask.

Cage Furniture

In nature, monitors and tegus often have a home burrow, or crevice, or hollow trunk to which they regularly return after foraging and at night. They are more secure in captivity when such provision is made. Although a custom box can be provided, even a simple closed cardboard box with an entrance hole provides security for your lizard. We actually prefer two hiding boxes, one warm and one cooler.

9

HOW-TO:
Make a Quasi-Natural Outdoor Cage

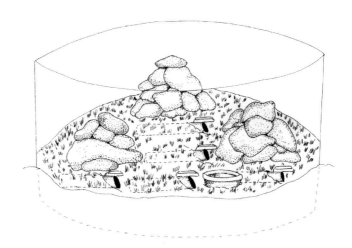

Outdoor monitor ring.

In southwest Florida we were very successful in breeding several species of small monitors in outside, quasi-natural facilities.

The cages were circular, of 8 to 10 foot (2.5–3.2 m) diameter, simple, and relatively inexpensive.

The walls were made from a strip of 3 foot (1 m) high aluminum sheeting sunk one foot (.3 m) into the ground. We found that the easiest way to outline and sink the sheeting was to use a posthole digger attached to a 4.5 foot (1.3 m) length of twine. The other end of the twine was noosed loosely around a post tapped into the ground where the center of the cage was to be. By keeping the posthole digger at the outer limit of the twine, it was a relatively simple matter to dig the foot-deep (.3 m) trench needed for the aluminum. No footer was needed. The aluminum sheeting was then set into the trench, leveled (this can be painstaking), and the two ends riveted together. The trench was then filled on both sides, with particular care given to the inside perimeter. Once the filling of the trench was complete, the cage was essentially done. The small diameter terra-cotta drainage pipes were then buried, pyramids of stones placed strategically, water supplied, and the lizards introduced. In our area (Lee County, Florida) these cages worked well, and since predators were not common, required no tops. Where either or both winged and four-footed predators (hawks, crows, cats, raccoons, opossums) are common, a top must be made for these open-air cages. The top can be framed from 1 × 2s (2.5 × 5 m) and covered with ¼-inch (.6 cm) mesh hardware cloth.

In our outside cages we provide either hollowed limbs or, in quasi-natural cages, rock piles (small species) and/or a labyrinth of buried pipes that double in the winter as hibernacula.

The floor covering of your indoor cage can consist of any number of items. Newspaper, wrapping paper, Astroturf, indoor/outdoor carpeting, cypress or aspen shavings or mulch (never cedar; it can be toxic to your lizard), or even rabbit food (compressed alfalfa pellets) are all ideal. In a room-sized cage (or the room itself), a linoleum covering is often used. The papers, shavings, and rabbit food can be discarded when soiled; the carpets can be washed, dried, and replaced, and the linoleum mopped.

Many persons have found that their monitors and tegus will repeatedly defecate in a particular area of their cage. Some specimens defecate in their water dishes, but others will quickly adopt a kitty pan containing a little sand.

Small, but sturdy living trees make attractive additions to monitor and tegu cages. Hardy and tolerant species are the various fig trees (*Ficus* sp.) and dragon trees (*Dracaena* sp.—note that this plant genus is the same as the genus of the caiman lizard). Such trees will thrive when the cages are outside during warm weather, but don't fare as well in indoor conditions. Besides the obvious attractiveness of the trees, the foliage provides visual barriers appreciated by the lizards.

Plastic plants are a viable alternative. They can be washed as they become soiled. They are generally sturdy enough to bear up under considerable abuse, and you can simply staple the foliage where you want it.

Cage/Terrarium Cleanliness

In the wild, these lizards can move around, so the buildup of organic debris simply does not occur. To

A large monitor, such as this 6 foot long adult Australian lace monitor, V. varius, *would require a room-sized cage.*

maintain suitable cleanliness in captive conditions, you'll probably need to clean your monitor/tegu cage at least twice a week. Water may need even more frequent cleaning. Since carnivorous lizards produce smelly stools, the prompt cleaning is for your sake as much as for that of the lizard. It is important that you choose the substrate or floor covering that is both safest for the lizard and most easily cleaned and sterilized.

Recent concerns about *Salmonella*, a common genus of bacteria that can cause gastrointestinal inflammation or infection in humans, mean that you need to keep the cage—and your hands—clean, and dispose of all wastes so that they do not contaminate food preparation or eating areas.

Lighting and Heating

Depending on the species, monitors, the tegus, and their relatives have varied lifestyles. They may be arboreal and heliothermic, terrestrial and heliothermic, or semiaquatic and heliothermic.

Note that all three descriptions include the term "heliothermic." Heliothermic relates to the sun and the temperature. Monitors and tegus

Wood-frame wire cage with hasp on the door, and a door near the bottom to facilitate cleaning.

While you won't be able to provide the waterway, cliff face exfoliations, or desert shrubs for your lizards, you can provide the light and warm limb or a sandy area on which to sprawl. A limb with bark will be much easier for your lizard to climb and cling to than one that has been peeled.

An elevated basking branch that is of *at least* the diameter of your lizard's body will be readily used by most species. If the limb is elevated only slightly above floor level, even normally terrestrial species may utilize it extensively. If more than one lizard is present, more than one basking platform should be provided—each illuminated and warmed. The limbs must be securely affixed to prevent toppling.

From above direct the warming beams of one or two floodlight bulbs onto this perch. A temperature of 95–105°F (35–40.5° C) (measured on the top of the basking limb) should be created. Be certain to position the bulbs so your lizard cannot burn itself if it approaches the lamp. Currently we use large incandescent plant-growth bulbs for this purpose. However, "full-spectrum" incandescent bulbs have recently appeared in the pet market. Although to date, since UV rays are not emitted, these bulbs would be better termed "color-corrected" than "full-spectrum," we hope improvements will be made.

Light and warmth are mandatory for the long-term well-being of your heliothermic lizards. It is at a body temperature of 88–95°F (31–35°C) that many heliotherms are most active and disease-resistant. Certain desert-dwelling heliothermic lizards may optimally attain even higher body temperatures.

Is full-spectrum (UV emitting) lighting actually necessary to the well-being of your monitor or tegu? Well, perhaps not absolutely necessary, but the UV-A and UV-B emissions are beneficial, even when in only small amounts.

regulate their body temperatures by basking (thermoregulating) in the sunlight until the optimum body temperature is attained. At optimum, the lizards are most efficient at approaching any exigencies.

Whether kept indoors or out, your monitors and tegus will require adequate heat and light. You will need to duplicate a sunlit habitat within their cage or room. Monitors and tegus like to sprawl while basking. Arboreal species will position themselves lengthwise along a sturdy limb, drooping their legs and part of their tails over the sides. In the wild such basking stations are often above waterways into which the lizards may drop if startled. Rock-dwelling species often bask in the sunlight in front of a deep fissure or crevice into which they may dart if disturbed. Terrestrial arid-land dwellers are often encountered in or near concealing patches of shrubby vegetation.

UV-A helps promote natural behavior in reptiles (see cautions in handling, page 27) and UV-B controls the biosynthesis of vitamin D_3 in the reptile's skin. When natural biosynthesis occurs, it allows greater error in feeding supplements, and in some instances, obviate vitamin and mineral supplementation altogether.

Let's look at this in a little more detail.

Truthfully, when it comes to assessing the benefits of artificial UV emissions, the jury is still out. Many keepers of heliothermic lizards consider the use of full-spectrum lighting mandatory. Others, however, have kept and bred these various lizard species without ever using full-spectrum lighting. We are ambivalent on the subject, but have never considered *not* using full-spectrum lighting.

Lizards provided with full-spectrum lighting, especially UV-A, *do* seem to display more normal behavior than those not so provided. Since normalcy of specimens is what most of us involved in herpetoculture are striving for, we always suggest that full-spectrum fluorescent lighting be used in addition to the incandescent lighting already mentioned. To date the favorite among the fluorescent full-spectrum bulbs is "Vita-LITE." There are several new contenders, some which may actually have a little greater UV output. It is UV-A and UV-B rays that you are hoping to provide for your lizard. Even when a bulb is new, the amount of these rays emitted is low. To gain *any* advantage from the bulb your lizard must be able to bask within 6–12 inches (15–30 cm) of it. Typical of any fluorescent tube, Vita-LITE bulbs give off little heat, so the lizard will not be burned even if it basks virtually against the bulb. Position the fixture accordingly.

Although the true benefits to your lizard from artificial sources is conjectural, the benefit from one lighting

Caging accessories with tegu hiding under plastic plants.

source is not—and this source is as close as your back door.

Natural Sunlight

Natural unfiltered sunlight unquestionably provides the best possible lighting (and heat) for any heliothermic lizard. We earlier stressed that your cages always be able to pass through your doorways and be on casters. Here is why; it will allow you to move your lizards—still securely caged—outdoors on warm, sunny days. In most cases the casters will allow a single person to accomplish this otherwise unwieldy task. There is simply nothing better that you can do for your lizards.

Only cages constructed of wood and wire should be placed out in the sun. A glass terrarium not only filters out the UV, but a glass terrarium, even with a screen top, will intensify and hold heat. This can literally cook your lizards in just a few minutes, even on a relatively cool day! Be sure to provide a shaded area for your lizard even in the wood/wire cages.

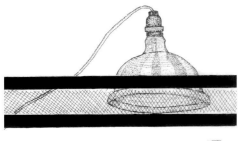

Dumeril's monitor draped over branch under heat lamp.

If you live in an area where it is absolutely impossible to get your lizard outside, perhaps you could allow it to bask in an opened window on hot summer days. Natural unfiltered sunlight from any vantage point will be of benefit.

More Heating Hints

It can be difficult on a cold northern winter day to provide adequate heat for your monitor or tegu—especially if it is a very large specimen in a proportionately large cage or if it is loose in its room.

Such devices as thermostatically controlled "hog blankets" (actually a livestock heating pad) can be purchased from many feed stores. Hot rocks can help, but keep a close eye on these to be sure they do not accidentally overheat and burn the lizard. Human heating pads, set on low, or ceramic space heaters will also help to either heat the lizard directly or to heat its cage or room. No matter which implements you use, be certain that they are thermostatically regulated to a suitable temperature, or that they are enclosed to prevent the lizard from coming in direct contact with them. Many severe reptile burns have occurred on particularly cold days when Herculean efforts are being made to provide sufficient heat. Don't let your lizard become a statistic!

Feeding and Watering Techniques

The Menu

Although the larger examples of many of these lizards probably do eat a considerable proportion of endothermic (warm-blooded) prey, few (if any) are specialist feeders on such items. Rather, most monitors and tegus are actually opportunistic feeders, eagerly accepting a wide variety of food items. Some species preferentially consume mollusks and crustaceans, and at least one monitor and most tegu species include a goodly amount of fruit in their diet.

Small species consume insects, other arthropods, smaller lizards, and, perhaps, the occasional nestling endotherm (a warm-blooded animal). Food items may be alive or in an advanced state of decomposition.

Larger species also consume insects, mollusks, crustaceans, and the eggs of birds and reptiles, but probably eat a greater overall percentage of vertebrate matter than their smaller relatives. Riverine and estuarine species may incorporate into their diet a great percentage of fish, baby crocodilians, turtles and their eggs, and other aquatic life. Carrion is also accepted.

The largest species of monitors (possibly excepting the slender, arboreal crocodile monitor of Irian Jaya) are formidable predators that are able to chase down and overpower small mammals and virtually anything else they happen across. As with the other groups, carrion also figures prominently in the diet of these largest of

lizards. In contrast, despite its size, the slender crocodile monitor probably feeds extensively on insects and nestling birds.

Diet caution: Although most monitors and tegus, including the highly insectivorous species, may adapt to a diet of pinky mice, today's reptilian veterinarians question the wisdom of such an obviously artificial diet. It seems that veterinarians are diagnosing a higher percentage of liver problems in lizards fed on an almost exclusive diet of pinky mice. A diet

Monitors are active and efficient predators. This baby Nile monitor, V. n. niloticus, is eating a goldfish.

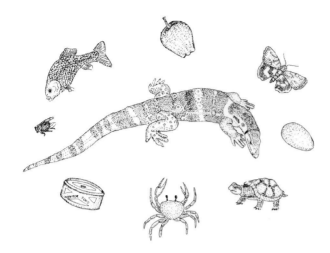
Monitor surrounded by potential food items.

Feeding

When you hear the crunch of bones caused when a large monitor or tegu grasps its prey, you know *immediately* that you need to avoid being bitten by this creature.

The jaws of monitors and tegus are strong, and the teeth are either sharp (occasionally serrate) for cutting or molariform for crushing.

Keepers often enjoy feeding their tegus and monitors by hand, citing their animals as "tame," and "trustworthy." This is almost a sure way to eventually sustain a severe bite. After handling the prey, your hands will smell and taste like the prey. Since monitors determine what's good to eat (most things) or what's not (almost nothing) by scent, taste, and sight, a hand that smells like a mouse or rat will probably be considered a mouse or a rat. Do not take the risk. Either place the food in a feeding dish or offer it on very long, blunt-tipped tongs.

Feeding hatchlings: Hatchling and baby monitors kept at optimally warm temperatures can eat from one to several fuzzy mice every second day. Crickets, mealworms, grasshoppers, roaches, and canned foods can also be offered and will usually be accepted. Prekilled food animals should be offered whenever possible.

Mid-sized monitors, (one-quarter to one-half grown) may be fed twice weekly, offering one to several small to medium prekilled mice at each feeding. Continue to offer insects and canned food. Some monitors will eagerly accept prekilled hatchling chicks.

Adult monitors may be fed from one to several large prekilled mice or suitably sized rats twice weekly. Prekilled chicks, large insects, and canned food should also be offered.

Tegus should be offered fare similar to food for like-sized monitors, plus an assortment of fruit.

exclusively of crickets has also been allied with liver disorders.

The Philippine Gray's monitor is the only monitor known to incorporate a high percentage of vegetable matter in its diet. Figs and other fruits are eagerly accepted.

Our tip: We have always considered a varied diet the best for all lizards. Crickets, grasshoppers, beetles, cockroaches, suitably sized mice, fish, crabs, crayfish, and prepared foods (Zoo-Med and Hill's A/D are manufacturers) should all be offered.

Tegus: In general, tegus eat much the same foods as monitors. The big difference is in the amount of vegetation tegus incorporate into their diet. As with captive monitors, a variety of food items is always the best choice.

Caiman lizards: Less is known about the true dietary needs of the caiman lizards. Once thought to feed exclusively on gastropod and bivalve mollusks, these large partially aquatic lizards have also been observed eating insects. Captives have eaten fish and canned cat foods.

Feeding prekilled rodents and chicks is not only humane, but will preclude the possibility of the lizard's being injured by its prey.

The amount of food offered should be based on how active your lizard is. The amount should also be varied as necessary, offering more if the lizard looks thin and less if chronic obesity is a problem.

Force-feeding: It may occasionally be necessary to force-feed ill or severely debilitated monitors and tegus. The item force-fed should be small and easily digested. Canned dog food, cat food, or monitor food moistened with Gatorade may be fed by stomach tube; be certain that you do not put the tube down the windpipe. Gatorade moistened pinky mice with the body cavity punctured may be gently forced down the lizard's throat. Overfeeding a debilitated lizard will surely cause regurgitation. A small meal, once every two days at first, then once a day as the lizard's condition improves, will be sufficient. Meal size can be slowly increased as the lizard regains its health. Temperature, stress-free housing, and illumination should be retained at round-the-clock optimum during sickness.

Insects: Catching Your Own

Netting insects from insecticide free areas is not only a viable option during the warmer months of the year, it also provides a supply of the healthiest insects possible for your lizards. To retain their food value, the insects must be eaten by the lizards within an hour or two after being collected. The type of insects you gather will vary according to the habitat through which you net. Netting through open fields should provide you with a series of grasshoppers, locusts, crickets, and a few other varieties. When netting through shrubby areas, you will usually find a preponderance of caterpil-

Sweep net for gathering insects.

lars, leafhoppers, and similar insects. Most of these will be fine for your lizards, and those that are noxious will usually be rejected by the lizards after one quick bite.

Insects can also be collected around a porch and beneath street lights at night. This method of collecting is often more tedious, but on "good" nights may be immensely productive. June beetles and other scarabs and moths are the forms most commonly collected during these nocturnal forays. Big diving beetles and bugs may be encountered in some numbers. These creatures have piercing mouthparts that can injure both you and the lizards. We do not collect these species.

Insects: Purchasing or Raising

It is important that you feed your varanids and teiids only the most nutritious food insects. Unless an insect is continually fed a nutritious diet (gut-loaded), it will provide little food value for your lizards. Maintaining your insects in top-notch health should be a main concern of any herpetoculturist.

17

Many monitors and teiids, like this small Amazonian black and yellow tegu, Tupinambis teguixin, *enjoy an occasional egg.*

The term "gut-loading" refers to feeding your insects an abundance of highly nutritious foods immediately before they are offered as food to your lizards. Potatoes alone won't do the job. Calcium, vitamin D_3, fresh fruit and vegetables, fresh alfalfa and/or bean sprouts, honey, and vitamin/mineral-enhanced (chick) laying mash are only a few of the foods that may be considered for gut-loading insects. A commercially prepared gut-loading diet has only recently reached the pet marketplace.

Many types of insects normally fed to your monitors, tegus, and relatives are commercially available. It may be your preference to buy these commercially available insects. Certainly this is less time-consuming than breeding

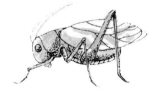
The gray cricket (Acheta domesticus).

your own insects, and these insects are available year-round. If you breed your own insects you can assure that the highest diet is continually fed the insects. Even if procuring the insects commercially you should feed them the best diet possible.

Crickets: The gray cricket (*Acheta domesticus*), is now bred commercially by the millions both for fishing bait and for pet food. Other species are readily collected in small numbers beneath debris in fields, meadows, and open woodlands. All species of crickets are an ideal protein source for your lizards.

Gray crickets are now so inexpensive that few hobbyists breed them. If you need only a few, they can be purchased from local pet shops. If you are feeding numerous insectivorous lizards, purchase your crickets from wholesale producers that advertise in fishing or reptile magazines. Prices are quite reasonable when crickets are purchased in multiples of 1,000.

Feed your crickets a good mold-free and varied diet and sprinkle the food with calcium/D_3 for the benefit of the lizards to which the crickets are fed. Crickets are cannibalistic if crowded or underfed. While crickets are able to metabolize most of their moisture requirements from fruit and vegetables, they will also appreciate a water source. Crickets will drown easily if they are given a plain, shallow dish of water. Instead, place cotton balls, a sponge, or even pebbles or aquarium gravel in the water dish. These will give the crickets sufficient purchase to climb out when they fall in.

Keep crumpled newspapers, the tubes from rolls of paper towels, or other such hiding areas in the crickets' cage. We prefer the paper towel tubes, for they can be lifted and the requisite number of crickets shaken from inside them into the cage or a transportation jar. This eases handling the fast-moving, agile insects. A tightly covered 20-gallon (76 L) long tank will temporarily house 1,000 crickets. Provide a substrate of sawdust, soil, vermiculite, or other such medium. This must be changed often to prevent excessive odor from the insects.

Grasshoppers/locusts (*Locusta* sp. and *Shistocerca* sp. in part): Although migratory and other locusts are not available in the United States, they are widely used as reptile foods in European and Asian countries. These can be bred or collected. Grasshoppers can be field-collected in the United States by the deft wielding of a field net. However, grasshoppers are fast and may be difficult to collect.

Caution: In some southern areas large, slow grasshoppers called "lubbers" may be found. Many of these have a brightly colored (often black and yellow or red) nymphal stage that can be fatally toxic if eaten. The tan and buff adults seem to be less toxic but their use as a food item is not suggested.

Waxworms (*Galleria* sp.): The "waxworm" is really the caterpillar, the larval stage of the wax moth that frequently infests neglected beehives. These are available commercially from many sources and are ideal food for small monitors and dwarf tegus. Check the ads in any reptile and amphibian magazine for wholesale distributors. Some pet shops and bait shops also carry waxworms. If you buy wholesale quantities of waxworms, you will need to feed them. Chick laying mash, wheat germ, honey, and yeast mixed into a syrupy paste will serve adequately as the diet for these insects.

Giant mealworms (*Zoophobas* sp.): These are the larvae of a South American beetle. They are rather new in the herpetocultural trade and at present, their ready availability is being threatened in the United States by the Department of Agriculture. This is

The grasshopper.

unfortunate, for *Zoophobas* have proven to be of great value to reptile breeders.

Although they are still available in many areas of the United States and virtually all over Europe and Asia, it would seem prudent for American herpetoculturists to breed their own.

Zoophobas can be kept in quantity in shallow plastic trays containing an inch (2.5 cm) or so of sawdust. To breed these mealworms, place one in each of a series of empty film canisters or other similar small containers that contains some sawdust, bran, or oats. The containment tends to induce pupation. After a few days the worm will pupate, eventually metamorphosing

Because snails figure prominently in the diet of the caiman lizard, Dracaena guianensis, *this species may be difficult to acclimate to captivity.*

The larvae of giant mealworms may be housed communally.

into a fair-sized black beetle. The beetles can be placed together for egg laying in a plastic tub containing a sawdust substrate and some old cracked limbs and twigs. The female beetles deposit their eggs in the cracks in the limbs. The beetles and their larvae can be fed vegetables, fruits, oat, and bran. The mealworms will obtain all of their moisture requirements from the fresh vegetables and fruit.

You can keep two colonies rotating to assure that you have all sizes of the larvae you will need to offer your various monitors and tegus. Although giant mealworms seem more easily digested by the lizards than common mealworms, neither species should be fed exclusively.

Mealworms (*Tenebrio molitor*): Long a favorite of neophyte reptile and amphibian keepers, mealworms should be just a part of your lizard's diet. These insects are easily kept and bred in plastic receptacles containing bran for food (available at your local livestock feed store). A potato or an apple will supply needed moisture. It takes no special measures to breed these insects.

Roaches: Although these can be bred, it is nearly as easy to collect roaches as needed. Roaches, of one or more species, are present over much of the world. Commercial breeders often concentrate on such large and "exotic" roach species as the Madagascar hissing and the tropical American giant. The size of the roach proffered must be tailored to the size of the lizard being fed.

Caution: Do not feed your lizards roaches from areas or habitations where insecticides are used!

Mice and Rats: To Purchase or Breed

Both mice and rats may be purchased—either alive or prekilled—from pet shops and/or commercial rodent breeders. We prefer to purchase the rodents we need, prekilled and frozen in bulk lots. Rodent suppliers often advertise in the classified sections of the various reptile and amphibian magazines. Local herpetology clubs, museums, nature centers, or biology departments may be able to direct you to local commercial sources. Do remember that it is much less costly to ship frozen rodents than to ship live ones.

Rodents are easily bred. A single male to 2 or 3 females in a 10-gallon (38 L) tank (or a rodent breeding cage) will produce a steady supply of babies that can be fed to your growing monitor, tegus, and their relatives. Do not use cedar bedding for rodents. The phenols contained in cedar can be harmful to the reptiles to which the rodents are fed. We suggest that you use aspen (our first choice) or pine shavings.

Feed your rodents either a "lab-chow" diet that is specifically formulated for them or a healthy mixture of seeds and vegetables. Fresh water must be present at all times.

Except that their caging should be larger, rats can be raised in much the same manner as mice. Rats do not breed as quickly as mice, and take longer to mature. Rats are an excellent staple (but not exclusive) food for larger monitors.

Vitamin/Mineral Supplements

Even with a well-rounded diet, it is unquestionably best to occasionally supplement your lizard's diet with vitamin/mineral additives. Those supplements most recommended supply calcium at a ratio of at least two to one over phosphorus. Vitamin D_3 is also an important additive.

An excess of Vitamin A in your reptile's diet can be detrimental.

Vitamin D_3 is essential to reptiles and amphibians. D_3 aids in the metabolizing of calcium. While D_3 can be synthesized in adequate amounts from an average diet if your specimens have access to natural sunlight, lesser amounts of UV-B will necessitate the addition of supplemental D_3. This holds true even with the much lauded full-spectrum lighting. Although full-spectrum illumination is definitely better than no illumination, the rays emitted by bulbs that are presently available are weak at best. Efficacy is lessened with bulb age. For your heliothermic lizards to get any benefit from the bulbs they must be both new and positioned very close to the lizard.

Supplemental calcium is always recommended. Exactly how much is necessary remains speculative. Rapidly growing baby and immature lizards most certainly have a higher calcium requirement than adults. Specimens recovering from rickets or metabolic bone disease will need more calcium than healthy specimens.

Phosphorus is almost always amply present in the normal diet of captive lizards, so many experienced and successful keepers and breeders recommend the augmentation of the calcium alone. At our facility we have used both the additives that supply only calcium and vitamin D_3 and additives containing a broader spectrum of ingredients. We can fault neither nor recommend one more strongly than the other. There are several excellent and commercially available calcium additives available at both your pet store and your veterinarian.

The vitamin/mineral supplements that we have used over the years are Osteo-Form and Rep-Cal.

Osteo-Form (calcium and phosphorus with vitamins) is a product of Vet-A-Mix, Inc. of Shenandoah, Iowa; it contains about twice as much calcium as phosphorus. This is an excellent ratio of these two indispensable products. Osteo-Form also contains a high amount of vitamin A and lesser amounts of vitamin D_3 and vitamin C.

Although this product contains more vitamin A than many herpetoculturists prefer, we have been very happy with the results produced by Osteo-Form. It is usually available from veterinarians, feed stores, and some pet shops.

Rep-Cal is calcium and vitamin D_3 with no phosphorus. It is a product of Rep-Cal Research Labs of Los Gatos, California.

Dosage: How much should you offer and how frequently? For adults, meaning those longer than three feet (1 m), add a pinch of the powder over their food twice weekly. For rapidly growing younger lizards add a small pinch of the powdered vitamin daily.

Monitors, tegus, and their relatives having unlimited access to natural unfiltered sunlight will not require as many vitamin/ mineral supplements as will those lizards maintained under artificial lighting.

Watering and Hydration Techniques

Some monitors get large. By large, we mean those monitors in the size range of the Nile and Asian—those that attain or exceed six feet (2 m) in length and are heavy of body. To be even relatively comfortable, these big lizards need a bathtub-sized water receptacle. Some specimens that are particularly large in either length or girth may be

Many monitors, like this baby Nile, V. n. niloticus, *are persistently aquatic. Captives enjoy large water containers.*

species, such as the savanna and white-throated monitors, will do quite well with just a sizable dish of drinking water and an occasional dip in your bathtub. But access to water should be always provided for water-oriented monitor species.

Water dishes should be available at all times for all species of monitors and tegus. Even desert forms that in nature may not have opportunity to drink every day, will, when captive, drink frequently and copiously.

All water dishes should be secured in place. This will prevent a boisterous monitor from overturning the dish, a feat at which monitors are particularly adept.

Misting: Persistently arboreal species may prefer to drink from the droplets on freshly misted leaves. For these, misting should be done daily. This is especially important in combating dehydration in newly imported and stressed representatives of particularly slender monitor species that come from humid forested habitats. Among these are the emerald and black tree monitors. When you mist, aim the mister so the water falls down onto the leaves and the lizard. Make sure that the slender hatchlings of Asian water, Nile, and other monitor species that originate from riparian habitats have enough access to water, both for drinking and swimming.

Keeping the provided water clean and the receptacle cleanable is as important as actually *providing* the water. While the cleaning of the small water bowl needed to accommodate a baby monitor is relatively simple, keeping a clean water supply for a seven-foot long, beer-keg diameter Asian water monitor is a whole different story. Necessarily, the container is immense, the volume of water is great, and if the monitor has defecated in it, cleaning is difficult. The most satisfactory method of draining

severely constrained even in a water container of this size. Because monitors are of tropical and subtropical origin, their water, no matter the volume, should be warm. We have found from 80 to 85°F (27–29°C) to be suitable.

How do you drain, sterilize and refill a bathtub-sized water receptacle? Truthfully, this can become an arduous and onerous task—and your ability to easily accomplish the necessary maintenance, including a sustained warm temperature of water in a container of this size, should be a main concern when you're considering the purchase of any monitor. Some and refilling large containers of water is to have them plumbed into the home water and drainage systems. Although the initial expense may be considerable, over time you will truly appreciate the convenience. The alternative is a frequent changing, pail by pail, followed by a difficult to accomplish sterilizing, rinsing, and refilling.

Watering Techniques for Tegus

Except for the two species of caiman lizards, genus *Dracaena*, which are strongly aquatic, the tegus are terrestrial. Neither the dwarf tegus of the genus *Callopistes* nor the true tegus of the genus *Tupinambis* require more than a shallow drinking container of suitable size. None of the lizards in these two latter genera are prone to taking the long soaks that typify so many of the monitors.

In contrast to the tegus, however, the caiman lizards are found in riverine situations. From slowly moving, heavily vegetated water, these large teiids often crawl out on to mats of emergent vegetation, overhanging trees, and riverine debris to bask and dry. Captives appreciate and fully utilize large water tubs. If the water is of sufficient depth, caiman lizards may submerge for long periods—sometimes days—occasionally tipping their snouts upwards through the surface to breathe.

Hydration Chamber

The benefits of hydration chambers have long been appreciated by zoos and other public institutions. They are only now coming into general use by private herpetoculturists and hobbyists. The term "hydration chamber" is merely a way of saying "rain chamber." Such a chamber can be of immense value to a dehydrated tegu or monitor. In fact, the prompt use of this receptacle can make the difference between life and death for

Misting a monitor.

freshly imported slender, easily dehydrated species such as the emerald and black tree monitors. A week or so of nearly perpetual high humidity interspersed with periodic mistings should do much to stabilize and rehydrate the lizards. Only warm, natural rains would be better. You can buy these chambers or make your own.

Making your own: A hydration chamber can be constructed of wire

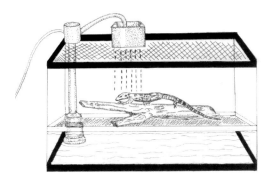

Homemade hydration system.

23

mesh over a wood frame, or of an aquarium equipped with a circulating water pump and a top that is a screen or perforated Plexiglas. If you are fortunate enough to live in a warm climate where the cage can be placed outdoors, a mist nozzle can be placed on the end of a hose, affixed over the cage, and fresh water run through this for an hour or more a day.

If indoors, the cage can be placed on top of or inside of a properly drained utility tub and the fresh water system used. It is imperative that the drain system be adequate and kept free of debris if this system is used indoors. A secondary (backup) drain (just in case...) might do much to guarantee your peace of mind.

In contained systems, a circulation pump can force water from the tank itself through a small diameter PVC pipe into which a series of lateral holes has been drilled, or merely brought up to the top of the tank and allowed to drip through the screen or perforated Plexiglas. It is imperative that the water in self-contained systems be kept immaculately clean and lukewarm.

Handling

Many monitors and tegus can become tame and trustworthy if obtained young, and given careful, gentle, and persistent handling. At one herpetological meeting we attended, a young lady arrived toting under one arm one of the biggest savanna monitors we have ever seen, and under the other arm what was certainly the largest black and white tegu we had ever seen. She had had both from babies, expended oodles of care and affection on the animals, and the results were gratifying.

Some species tend to tame more readily than others, but some examples of even the more traditionally irascible species will become tame. Of the monitors, the African savanna and the Asian water monitor tame rather readily. The first of these two is perhaps the commonest monitor in the pet store trade; the latter was once commonly seen, but is no longer so. The African Nile monitor, a very pretty black and yellow species that *is* still common in the pet trade, has a well-deserved reputation for being one of the more difficult species to tame. While some babies do tame, most remain flighty and ready to bite. If they are larger than hatchling size when imported from the wild, they are even more difficult to tame.

Thick welder's gloves and a long-sleeved shirt will provide you with a certain advantage when beginning your taming efforts with any sizable monitor or tegu.

Of the tegus, the Amazonian black and yellow tegu, the species most commonly available, is also the most difficult to tame. The larger black and white and the red tegus are comparatively easygoing animals but are expensive and available only occasionally from specialty dealers.

Monitors and tegus that are unaccustomed to handling have a remarkable set of defensive tactics to advise you that they much prefer to be left alone. Not all of the tactics are used by all species (some seem not to slap with their tails, for instance), but those mechanisms that *are* used may be used singly or in combination.

Holding a tame white-throated monitor.

Many monitors held in this manner will severely scratch your arm. It is best to immobilize both fore and rear limbs. Pictured is an immature Australian perentie, V. giganteus.

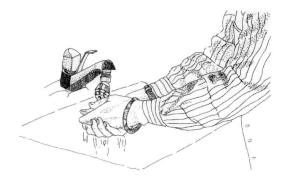

Hands should be washed thoroughly after handling a lizard.

Monitors first rely on escape to avoid enemies, either real or imagined. If, however, they are cornered and unable to flee, body language—intimidation of an enemy through posturing that includes laterally flattening and arcing the body, expanding the throat, lolling the tongue out—is the next line of defense. During this, the tail is often arced and lashed with unerring accuracy. While this may seem ludicrous when it is indulged in by a small monitor, it is no laughing matter when the tail of a large monitor connects with your hand, arm, leg, or—if you happen to be bending toward the lizard—your face.

Like monitors, tegus would prefer flight to confrontation with enemies. However, if cornered, tegus tend to inflate their body, arc it upwards, and inflate their throat. They bite (*very* effectively), scratch (less effectively than many monitors), void their intestinal contents on a captor, but tend not to slap with their tail.

The tail of a tegu can autotomize and regenerate, to a degree. If the tail of a monitor is broken, it does not regenerate.

Biting: This sounds straightforward enough. While the jaws of even a moderate-sized monitor are formidably strong, not all monitor species are predisposed to biting when handled. However, those that are not inveterate biters are often the smaller species that couldn't hurt you severely if they did bite. But when you get to the size range of the green and black tree monitors, both of which are perfectly ready to bite when disturbed, to hold on with bulldog tenacity once they have bitten, and to clamp down more tightly at every movement you make to extricate yourself, you can be hurt—and hurt badly. Remember, these are fairly small monitors, species that have a SVL of only about 10 inches (25 cm). You absolutely don't want to get bitten by one of the larger monitor species. Coupled with the power of the bite is the worry that the teeth and jaws of many monitor species may carry substantial quantities of bacteria. This is especially so if the lizard has been feeding on well-ripened carrion. Wash and disinfect any wounds carefully and thoroughly!

Wild tegus bite readily and hard when cornered, but often do not retain their grip with the tenacity of a monitor. We have never had a tegu fail to release its grip if it was placed upon the ground.

Scratching: Again, this designation sounds straightforward, but with many monitor species it is anything but simple. A carelessly grasped monitor, especially of an arboreal type with sharply recurved claws, will display a twist of efficiency to the art of scratching that is sure to amaze the first-time recipient of the technique. Unless prevented from doing so, when grasped, a monitor will twist its ventral surface against your arm, spread its rear legs widely, tightly grasp your arm, dig in its claws, and rake your skin. Wash and disinfect the welts and wounds carefully and thoroughly! Monitor claws can transmit bacteria to the wounds.

The claws of the largely terrestrial tegus are not strongly recurved. Tegus can and will scratch their captors in their attempts to escape, but are less effective in these efforts than many monitors.

Voiding the contents of the intestinal tract: Many monitors are not at all reluctant to add insult to injury. While they are biting you or raking you with their claws, leaving welts or bleeding scratches, these lizards may also void a copious amount of fluid and feces from their intestinal tract. At best this is harmless, but messy, smelly, and disconcerting! However, it can also cause infection if it enters an open wound. In all cases, thoroughly wash and disin-

fect your hands, arms, and additional splashed areas of your body. If you are in doubt, consult a physician.

Although a frightened, carelessly restrained tegu will void, these lizards are less apt to do so than most monitors.

Natural sunlight: Owners who have raised and tamed their monitors and tegus indoors under artificial lighting may see a dramatic change for the worse in the attitude of their lizards when they are provided with natural sunlight. However, the disposition of some of these lizards seems not to change at all even when in natural sunlight, and all will revert to their former state of complacency (if applicable) when moved back indoors.

Some of these lizards (tegus, especially) may be most savage during the breeding season, and females are often especially so as the egg deposition date nears.

As it grows, Eric Pierce's hatchling Nile monitor may become more difficult to handle.

HOW-TO:
Handle Your Monitor or Tegu

To a degree, you can consider the feistiness shown by a *freshly imported* monitor or tegu as a barometer of the lizard's overall health. If a newly imported monitor or tegu *does not* respond defensively to your overtures, it is probably a sick or weak lizard that you should not consider purchasing. In most cases, with lizards in these two groupings, belligerence equates, to some degree, with stamina and health.

A fully warmed monitor or tegu will be more difficult to approach and handle than a cool or cold specimen, simply because warmed specimens move more quickly and decisively. A monitor or tegu warmed by natural unfiltered sunlight will be more difficult yet. However, an optimally warmed monitor is more apt to try to escape than to bite. The reverse will often be true of a cool/cold monitor or tegu. As if recognizing that its suboptimal body temperature will cause it to be slower and less agile, a cool monitor or tegu is more apt to stand its ground, jaws gaping, in biting readiness.

How does one handle such an animal—an animal that will wriggle, squirm, bite, and scratch when grasped? The basic response must be "carefully—*very* carefully!"

The body and neck of very small wild specimens can be encircled with the fingers of one hand.

The head should be immobilized in the same manner as you would immobilize the head of a snake.

Larger wild monitors and tegus will require a coordinated two-handed capture technique. With one hand it will be necessary to encircle the neck, the head, and the forelimbs, while simultaneously immobilizing the rear limbs with the other hand. It would be best if the tail could be immobilized with a third hand, but lacking this appendage, grasping the tail between your arm and body may save you some welts, or at least some discomfort. Tail immobilization is more important with large monitors than with tegus.

Even when handling large monitors and tegus that seem perfectly tame, always watch for signs of irascibility. This is especially so if handling or husbandry techniques are changed. Being prepared for any eventuality may well save you from an uncomfortable encounter.

Merely handling your monitor or tegu is very different from trying to tame it. If you hope to accomplish taming the lizard, we strongly suggest that you begin with the youngest specimen available and work with it— preferably several times daily. Select one of the more easily tamed species, and if you have your choice of several similar ones, choose a healthy appearing, relatively unaggressive individual. When nearing or handling your lizard, always move slowly and nonthreateningly.

If your lizard will allow you to touch it without threatening to bite, do so without gloves. If it is more aggressive, wear gloves,

even if they are thin. Your hope is to gradually accustom your lizard to being touched, lifted, and carried. You may choose to first merely rub its nape or dorsum gently. When the lizard tires of this it will inflate its body or dash away. Desist, then try again in an hour or two. Next, gently lift the lizard. Grasp it tightly enough so it can't squirm free, but not so tightly that it feels incapacitated and threatened. Next allow it to walk from hand to hand, holding the lizard close enough to a horizontal surface so if it falls or jumps it will not hurt itself. Go through the same procedure day after day, several times a day if possible. Eventually most monitors will lose their fear of you, and you will be able to easily handle them. However, there are always the few that will resist your most persistent and gentle overtures and simply remain nervous and untrusting. If you can be satisfied with a nonhandleable monitor or tegu, keep and enjoy the lizard. If not, divest yourself of it and begin the process anew.

A word of caution: Not everyone likes lizards—especially large lizards. The pathway to regulations and restrictions is often opened when someone is frightened by an unthinking or uncaring owner of a monitor or tegu. Persons who do not wish to encounter these animals have that right. Adverse interactions can only lead to additional regulatory laws. Be a responsible pet owner. Use care and courtesy at all times.

Regulations about the ownership of large reptiles may already be in effect in your community. Care and be aware.

Health

Diet-Related Health Problems

Although varanids and teiids seem less prone than many lizards to diet-related health problems, these can and do occur. All can be avoided (and sometimes corrected) by providing a correct diet. The four most commonly encountered problems are metabolic bone disease (including rickets and demineralization), liver dysfunction, vitamin/mineral imbalance, and elimination problems (constipation or diarrhea).

Our discussion of these problems is in no way intended to supplant the diagnoses and treatments offered by your qualified reptile veterinarian. A *qualified* reptile veterinarian can be your best friend during times of trouble. The vet's recommendations should be followed to the letter.

Metabolic Bone Disease (MBD)

What is MBD, and is it preventable?

In simplified terms, MBD is the withdrawal of bone calcium to maintain its needed level in the blood. The cause is improper diet, and yes, it is entirely preventable.

A lizard suffering from MBD is usually inactive and, except for a plumpness in its limbs, appears thin. Sometimes the jawbones become shortened and the face looks chubby. That "plumpness" is your cue. It signifies a major health problem, one where the calcium is leached from the bony tissue and replaced by a fibrous tissue. Your animal needs immediate veterinary care.

The technical names for metabolic bone disease are "nutritional secondary hyperparathyroidism" and "fibrous osteodystrophy." Common names for the problem include rickets and demineralization. The disease is most commonly seen in lizards that have been fed a diet rich in phosphorus and deficient in calcium or that are unable to properly absorb and metabolize their calcium because of a lack of vitamin D_3.

To exist, your monitor or tegu needs a certain level of blood calcium. When the level of blood calcium drops below a certain percentage, the parathyroid glands begin the complex process of withdrawing calcium from the bones to the blood. As the bones lose their rigidity, parts become replaced with a fibrous tissue and deformities occur.

The preventive agent for MBD is calcium. The calcium/phosphorus balance of diet and additives needs to be monitored carefully. Food items and supplements should offer a ratio of two parts calcium to one part phosphorus.

Your lizard also needs vitamin D_3 to absorb calcium. Vitamin D_3 intake needs to be supplemented, especially when your specimen does not have regular (daily, or at least weekly) access to direct unfiltered sunlight. (The natural sunlight induces normal D_3 synthesis.)

Lizards with unlimited access to natural *unfiltered* sunlight require a lesser amount of D_3 and calcium additive than those with limited or no such access. Full-spectrum bulbs, although beneficial, produce only small amounts of the UV-A and UV-B rays so necessary to the synthesis and metabolism of vitamins and minerals by your monitors and tegus. Regular vitamin/mineral augmentation of the diet is very important.

Even when a diet provides sufficient calcium, if the phosphorus ratio is too high or D_3 is not present, MBD can and will occur. The debilitation is a long process through which your lizard will often continue eating and reacting "normally" until it is no longer able to do so.

MBD can be treated by the injections of a soluble calcium and vitamin D_3. The treatment will work for MBD in its early stages, and in some late stage cases.

The treatment begins with lab work to determine the actual blood calcium levels. Once the diagnosis of MBD is confirmed, your veterinarian will begin three days of treatment with injectable calcium and (often) oral vitamin D_3. Oral calcium may also be administered. Corrected diet will enable the lizard to maintain its health.

Vitamin/Mineral Imbalances

Throughout the text, the importance of vitamins and minerals in correct proportions has been stressed. Since this aspect is critically important, we will stress it again here.

1. Calcium is necessary for proper bone development and life itself. Ultraviolet rays promote vitamin D_3 synthesis, and allow reptiles to properly absorb and metabolize calcium. Natural sunlight is the best source for UV, but full-spectrum lighting provides a little.

2. Vitamin D_3 is necessary to help a reptile absorb and metabolize the necessary amounts of calcium. Too much D_3 will allow too much calcium to be absorbed; too little D_3 will retard calcium absorption.

3. Phosphorus, when offered at too high a level, can hinder the proper metabolizing of calcium.

4. Vitamin A is usually present in adequate amounts in the normal diet of your lizard. Vitamin A enhancements are seldom necessary.

5. Vitamin B is usually of no concern in carnivorous lizards eating a varied diet. Thiamine (B_1) imbalances (which cause nerve disorders) could occur if a preponderance of dead fish is fed. If detected early, this disorder is usually correctable.

6. Vitamin C is synthesized internally and also adequately present in balanced diets. A deficiency would manifest itself in hemorrhaging of the mucous membranes and bruising.

7. Vitamin D: The integral role of vitamin D_3 in the health of your lizard has already been discussed in detail.

8. Vitamin E deficiencies are diet-related. Feeding your varanids and teiids a healthy, varied diet will assure that no E-vitamin deficiencies occur.

Constipation and Diarrhea

The normal bowel movements of varanids and teiids vary remarkably in consistency. Normal movements are largely white with some dark coloration. The white portions are urinary solid wastes, called urates. The dark brown portions are feces. Those of a properly hydrated lizard will be moist, like a semiliquid jelly. Those of dehydrated specimens will be dry.

Bowel movements do not necessarily occur at regular intervals. The body temperature of your lizard will largely determine the speed with which digestion occurs. Cooler lizards will defecate less frequently than specimens kept at warmer temperatures.

If a monitor or tegu is kept too cool, the digestive process may either stop or be so inhibited that ingested foods spoil in the stomach. In extreme cases, the lizard may vomit these masses. Properly warm temperatures are mandatory for normal digestive processes to occur. An ideal daytime temperature range would be between 86 and 94°F (30–34°C). Slightly cooler daytime temperatures from 77–80°F (25–27°C) are permissible for short periods.

The failure of your lizard to defecate or pass urates may also result from a gastrointestinal impaction. The chances of this are heightened in monitors and tegus that are grossly overweight or very inactive. Impactions may be caused by ingested matter (pebbles, shavings, or kitty litter), or by abnormally dry stools (in dehydrated teiids). Again, proper hydration will preclude many problems.

A period of activity, such as a swim in a tub of tepid water, may induce defecation. Large immovable impactions may require veterinary intervention. Some impactions may respond to small amounts of softening agents or lubricants available from your pharmacy. Use milk of magnesia or Siblin—administered orally, or small amounts of petroleum jelly inserted rectally.

Fecal material that is not expelled has more and more moisture resorbed, and then normal bowel peristaltic motility cannot expel it. These stubborn impactions may require surgical removal.

Diarrhea is a condition in which your lizards produce abnormally loose stools. Occasional loose stools may be induced by a dietary change, in tegus, by the ingestion of moisture-laden fruit, by periods of stress, illness, or other such abnormal conditions. In most cases, this is nothing to worry about. Cutting back on fruit and/or adding items with a lower fat content will likely correct the looseness.

Intestinal worms and overgrowth of some species of gut bacteria can also cause diarrhea. Veterinary intervention is indicated in either case. The worms should be eradicated. The bacteria count can be lowered via antibiotic administration.

Mechanical Injury

Despite your every caution, monitors and tegus may sustain an injury. The lizards may find undreamed-of ways to lodge themselves against a heating lamp and get burned; a metal staple may break off and the lizard is cut or punctured by the jagged edge; or the lizard may get injured in the shipping process en route to the pet store. With animals, as with small children, you can adopt a corollary of Murphy's Law: they can get hurt when you least expect it. This section will help you deal with some of the more common traumatic incidents, such as burns, cuts, abrasions, rubbed noses, injured toes, clipping toenails, broken limbs, and skin-shedding problems.

Burns: Your captive lizard can be burned in any of several ways. The most frequent cause is prolonged contact with a cage heating or lighting element that is either malfunctioning or for which proper protection has not been installed.

Among others, "hot rocks," other heating units, and incandescent light bulbs have been implicated in superficial to severe burning incidents.

Burned areas are often discolored but usually not blistered. Treatment will depend upon the severity of the burn. Superficial burns will often require no treatment at all, but the cause must be corrected. Mild to moderate burns must be cleaned and antiseptic ointment applied, especially if the burn is oozing fluid. Severe burns will need vigorous medical treatment; your veterinarian should be consulted immediately. One of the problems you will encounter is the lizard's loss of appetite, combined with a great need for fluids and energy/calories for healing.

We are not proponents of hot rocks or heat-bricks or other similar ventrally oriented heating devices. Most monitors and tegus are heliotherms (basking species) that preferentially thermoregulate by basking in the sunlight until warm. They then move to a more shaded area so as not to overheat. They are designed to most efficiently absorb and evenly distribute warmth through their bodies when heated from above. This should not be construed as meaning that on cloudy days, or even at other times when they are cool, they will not happily rest on a warmed surface. They will! But we—and often they—feel that dorsal is better. It is for this reason that they regularly and readily utilize a lighted area warmed by a heat bulb.

Heat and other incandescent bulbs will need to be carefully placed, too. A high-wattage, heat-emitting bulb that is too close can burn.

If you are convinced that a ventral heater is necessary, we most readily recommend undertank heaters.

Cuts and Abrasions may be as diverse in severity as burns. The seriousness of either will determine the needed response. The cause of the

Covering an aquarium with paper so the monitor won't bang its snout.

injury will need to be immediately corrected. If the wound is dirty, clean it with soap and water; be sure to rinse well. For a minimal wound an over-the-counter antiseptic ointment will suffice. As with humans, if possible, the area needs to be protected from dirt until it heals. The problem is that commercial strip bandages either won't stick to lizard skin or they stick too well and you'll have problems in removal. Depending on where the injury is, you might be able to wrap a gauze bandage around the affected area and secure the bandage to itself with adhesive tape. A product called "New Skin" may work better than a bandage. For more serious wounds, veterinary assistance should be immediately sought.

Nose Rubbing is one of the most common abrasions and is one of the most difficult to correct. It is the direct result of escape efforts by your lizard and may be indulged in by either tame or wild specimens. It makes little difference to the lizards whether the cage is constructed of glass or wire (smooth or rough).

Nose rubbing by newly collected monitors and tegus or by specimens that have been used to "the run of the house" is self-explanatory. Nose rubbing by fearful wild lizards that are trying unsuccessfully to return to the wild is equally easily explained. Larger cages may lessen the problem by providing a greater feeling of security and more actual "freedom."

Covering at least three sides of the cage with opaque paper, cloth, or "contact paper" may also help alleviate the problem.

To prevent easily startled, extremely wild specimens from repeatedly reinjuring their snouts, it may be necessary to also cover the remaining side. However, in truth this is self-defeating, for it will prevent the lizards from ever becoming accustomed to motion and your presence. Another method, one that we prefer for extremely wild specimens, is to suspend a soft cloth barrier about two inches (5 cm) on the *inside* of the glass or wire sides of the cage. By coming in contact with the hanging cloth first, the specimen substantially lessens its impact with the cage side. For the side which you approach most frequently, the barricade can be suspended halfway up from the bottom. This way, the lizard can see you and yet avoid injury if it runs into the cage wall.

Toe Problems: Broken toes, torn-off toenails, and sharp claws are all frequently encountered when one keeps lizards. Toes may be broken during escape efforts, or if the lizard catches its claws inextricably in carpeting or in a narrow aperture. Sometimes humans cause this by stepping on the toe of an uncaged monitor or tegu. If the break is fresh and simple, the toe may often be splinted and saved. If the break is old and/or compound, amputation is usually preferred. Consult your veterinarian.

Torn-off toenails occur for the same series of reasons that breaks do. Merely apply an antiseptic ointment or powder and keep your lizard quiet until the bleeding stops. These injuries will often heal quickly without any additional procedures. However, if the toe becomes swollen or infected, consult your veterinarian.

Many monitors and some tegus are partially to extensively arboreal. To accommodate their climbing habits, their claws are sharp and recurved. In the wild, the normal activity of the lizard usually keeps the claws somewhat dulled. Since most captive monitors or tegus never have opportunity to climb and run extensively, it may be desirable to occasionally clip off the very tip of the claw. Often a two-person job, nail-trimming is easiest (especially if the lizard is large) if the specimen is firmly but gently

restrained and rolled onto its side with its belly facing the person who is to do the trimming. Using either human or pet nail clippers, it is then possible to carefully remove the tip of the claw. If the claws of baby lizards are carefully inspected, you can often see traces of venation at their cores. Care should be taken not to cut the claw so short that it bleeds. If bleeding does occur, apply a styptic and an antibiotic powder or salve.

Occasionally a constriction of fiber or even unshed skin on the toe can inhibit normal blood circulation. If unresolved, this can lead to the distal portion blackening as the tissue dies, dries out, and eventually drops off. Normally this is not accompanied by any swelling or infection, and, in fact, is seldom detected until it is too late to correct the problem. A periodic inspection of your lizard's toes for constricting fibers or rings of dried skin and their prompt and gentle removal if found can lessen the probability of a problem.

Broken Tails: The breaking of a tail is of different severity when it happens to a monitor than when it happens to a teiid.

Monitors have no fracture planes in the caudal vertebrae, and their tail will not regenerate if broken. The tail break may heal if splinted, or it may be necessary to have the tail amputated. Consult your veterinarian.

Although the breaking of a tail in an otherwise perfect teiid lizard can be disheartening, it is probably considered more serious by the keeper than the kept. The tails of teiid lizards are designed by Mother Nature to break if necessary. This is a defensive mechanism with considerable survival value. In some of the caudal (tail) vertebrae there is a weakened "fracture plane" to facilitate easy breakage. If, as frequently does happen, a predator grasps the lizard by the tail, the tail

Vertebrae with and without fracture plane.

breaks off and through convulsive wriggling, retains the predator's attention. Unless the break is well up on the basal portion of the tail, little bleeding accompanies the autotomization. Regeneration of the tail begins nearly immediately. The completeness and appearance of the regenerated tail depends upon numerous criteria. Among others are the age of the lizard, the area of the break, and whether or not the break was clean and complete or irregular and partial.

Tails broken beyond the center point of the tail usually regenerate more completely than those broken closer to the body. A clean, complete break will usually result in a more normally tapering, natural appearing regenerated member. With care (and luck) a partial break may heal in a natural position. Alternatively, the break may complete itself at a later date and heal askew; in some cases a second, abnormal-appearing tail may grow to join the first.

Tails of young teiids broken on their distal half seldom need attention. Tails of adults broken on their distal third are likewise not apt to require attention. The tails of both young and old broken closer to the body may require cauterization and/or suturing to staunch blood flow and quickly close the wound.

In all cases, clean the break with a dilute Betadine solution and keep the area clean.

Broken Limbs: The leg bones of monitors and tegus are strong and designed to withstand considerable stress without mishap. In the wild, one of these lizards with a broken limb would be easy prey. Arboreal monitors have been seen to drop several dozen feet from a tree limb where they were basking to both dry ground and water. After landing on the former they scuttled off at great speed, showing no evidence that the drop had affected them adversely. When landing in water they dive and swim to safety, again showing no ill effects from the powerful landing impact.

Therefore, if a captive monitor or tegu breaks its leg, it is *usually* either caused by an accident or indicative of another underlying problem such as metabolic bone disease (see page 29). In either case, splinting (and/or pinning, depending upon the severity and complexity of the break) will be necessary. Veterinary help should be sought immediately.

If the break was caused by an accident, steps should be taken to ascertain that the break does not have an opportunity to recur. If it is determined that the break was the result of calcium deficiency, the condition should be first stabilized with injectable calcium, then dietary corrections immediately made.

Infections: If kept in clean caging, neither monitors nor tegus are likely to develop infections, even from open wounds. It is when their quarters are allowed to become dirty or when the animals are stressed that infections are most likely to occur. If untreated, infections can literally and quickly overwhelm even an otherwise healthy specimen.

Abscesses, suppuration, discolorations, and other such abnormal signs may indicate either a localized or a systemic infection. Swollen limbs might mean metabolic bone disease, an equally serious problem which was covered earlier in this chapter. A veterinarian well versed in reptilian disorders should be consulted immediately. In some cases it may be necessary to obtain cultures to determine an effective treatment. In other cases the causative agents may respond quickly to broad-spectrum antibiotics (these will usually be injected for immediate action). When a monitor or tegu is profoundly ill, it generally doesn't eat, or will have trouble metabolizing food if it does eat. In all cases proper cleanliness of both lizard and cage are very important for recovery.

Shedding Problems: A monitor or tegu that walks around sporting large patches of exfoliating skin is apt to be perceived as a lizard with problems. Such is not usually the case.

Reptiles shed their skin to facilitate growth. This is natural. Unlike snakes, which are well known for their entire, inverted shed skins, most lizards shed their skin less neatly and in a patchwork manner. This, too, is natural—unless the skin adheres tightly and is not lost by the lizard within a day or two. Increasing the humidity in the cage and moistening your lizard's shedding skin will often help. A gentle tug by you on the edges may also help. It is important, however, that you not remove the flaking skin before it is ready to be removed. The newly forming skin beneath may be damaged if things are rushed.

Do spend a few moments checking your lizard after each shed. Ascertain that no rings of scales remain on the digits, tail, or elsewhere, where they may then dry and restrict circulation. Should you find such problems, remove the skin gently and promptly. It may be necessary to soak your lizard for a few minutes to promote softening and facilitate easy removal.

Several other diseases and maladies may rarely occur.

Mineralization of internal organs: This is caused by over-absorption of calcium, known as hypercalcemia. Treatment is both lengthy and expensive and requires about two weeks of monitoring by a veterinarian. Once the disease has been diagnosed and corrected it will be necessary for you to reduce both calcium and D_3 intake by your specimen. There is a fine line between too much and not enough calcium and vitamin D_3. Untreated or too far advanced, this disease can be fatal.

Hypoglycemia is an abnormal decrease in blood sugar. Stress or pancreatic dysfunction can be the causative agent. The stress factor is correctable; the pancreatic dysfunction, sometimes caused by an insulin-secreting tumor, usually is not.

Pathogens and Parasites

Ectoparasites: External parasites are less problematic to treat than endoparasites. Only ticks are seen with any regularity on monitors and tegus. These feed on the body fluids of their hosts.

Ticks are deflated and seedlike when empty, rounded and bladderlike when engorged. It is best if they are removed singly whenever seen. They imbed their mouthparts deeply when feeding, and if the ticks are merely pulled from the lizard, the mouthparts may break off in the wound. It is best to first dust the ticks individually with Sevin powder or to rub them with rubbing alcohol, then return a few minutes later and pull them gently off with a pair of tweezers.

Respiratory Disorders

Although well-acclimated, properly maintained monitors and tegus are not prone to respiratory ailments, stressed new imports, marginally healthy specimens, and those subjected to unnatural periods of cold (especially damp

The emaciated appearance of the savanna monitor pictured on the top indicates poor health (note the tick between the eye and ear opening). The savanna monitor on the bottom is bright-eyed and healthy.

cold) may occasionally be affected with "colds" or pneumonia. Some respiratory conditions may also be associated with depressed immunity brought about by a heavy endoparasite burden.

Respiratory ailments are initially accompanied by sneezing, lethargic demeanor, and unnaturally rapid, often shallow breathing.

As the respiratory infection worsens, rasping and bubbling may accompany each of your lizard's breaths. At this stage the infection is often critical and can be fatal.

It is mandatory that basking temperatures be elevated during treatment. Monitors and tegus are dependent upon outside heat sources for maintaining their metabolic rate. The warmer the surroundings, the better able the lizard is to digest its food and fight off diseases or injury.

As soon as a respiratory ailment is suspected, elevate the temperature of your lizard's basking area to about 100°F (37.7°C). Do not elevate the temperature of the entire cage to this level!

The ambient cage temperature should be 88–92°F (31–33°C). If the symptoms of respiratory distress do not greatly lessen within a day or two, do not delay any longer. Call your veterinarian and take your lizard for antibiotic treatment.

There are many "safe" drugs available, but some respiratory illnesses do not respond well to these. The newer aminoglycoside drugs are more effective, but correspondingly more dangerous. There is little latitude in dosage amounts and the lizard *must* be well hydrated to ensure against renal (kidney) damage. The injection site for aminoglycosides should be *anterior* to mid-body to *assure* that the renal-portal system is not compromised. Your veterinarian must be well acquainted with reptilian medicine to assure that the correct decisions are made.

Endoparasites: The presence of internal parasites in wild-caught monitors and tegus is a foregone conclusion. Among others that may be present are roundworms, pin worms, other nematodes, tapeworms, and a whole host of flagellate protozoans.

Although many persons feel blanket treatment of all imported specimens a necessity, we feel that whether or not the parasites are combated vigorously should depend on the behavior of each individual lizard. Certainly the problems created by endoparasitic loads in weakened lizards need to be addressed promptly. Since fecal exams will have to be performed to determine what the lizard is actually harboring in its gut, it is best to avail yourself of the services of a reptilian veterinarian, who will be best qualified to determine when and with what to treat the problem.

However, if the specimen in question is bright-eyed, alert, feeding well, and has a good color, you may wish to forego an immediate veterinary assessment. Endoparasitic loads can actually diminish if you keep the cage of your specimen scrupulously clean, thereby preventing reinfestation.

Gut and tissue strongyloid nematodes may be particularly persistent. To eradicate them often require a lengthy bout of purges. We have often wondered at what point a treatment becomes more of a burden for a specimen than the parasites actually are. In the case of strongyles, the answer seems to be a tossup. While an overload of strongyloid nematodes can cause chronic diarrhea, a small load of these parasites may cause no problems whatever. We feel that discrimination should be used by the veterinarian in determining whether or not to treat a given specimen.

Simply stated, the treatment for endoparasites involves administering a potentially toxic substance into the system of your lizard. Because of this, dosages of the drug(s) must be exact! It is very easy for a layperson unfamiliar with the conversion of the metric doses of medication to overmedicate or undermedicate a specimen. In the first case the result may be fatal.

In the latter case the effort will probably have been futile. Again, we strongly suggest you avail yourself of the services of a knowledgeable veterinarian.

Medications

Medical treatments for parasitism: Many varanids and teiids harbor internal parasites. This is especially so of wild-collected specimens. Because of the complexities of identification of endoparasites and the necessity to accurately weigh specimens to be treated and to measure drug dosages, the eradication of internal parasites is best left to a qualified reptile veterinarian. These are a few of the recommended medications and dosages. This information was provided to us by Richard Funk, DVM, a herpetoculturist and reptile disease specialist.

Amoebas and *Trichomonads:* 40–50 mg/kg of **Metronidazole** orally. The treatment is repeated in two weeks.

Dimetridazole can also be used but the dosage is very different. 40–50 mg/kg of Dimetrizadole is administered daily for five days. The treatment is then repeated in two weeks. All treatments with both medications are administered once daily.

Coccidia: Many treatments are available.

The dosages of **sulfadiazine, sulfamerazine,** and **sulfamethazine** are identical. Administer 75 mg/kg the first day, then follow up for the next five days with 45 mg/kg. All treatments orally and once daily.

Sulfadimethoxine is also effective. The initial dosage is 90 mg/kg orally to be followed on the next five days with 45 mg/kg orally. All dosages are administered once daily.

Trimethoprim-sulfa may also be used. 30 mg/kg should be administered once daily for seven days.

Cestodes (=Tapeworms): Several effective treatments are available.

Bunamidine may be administered orally at a dosage of 50 mg/kg. A second treatment occurs in 14 days.

Niclosamide, orally, at a dosage of 150 mg/kg, is also effective. A second treatment is given in two weeks.

Praziquantel may be administered either orally or intramuscularly. The dosage is 5–8 mg/kg and is to be repeated in 14 days.

Trematodes (Flukes):

Praziquantel at 8 mg/kg may be administered orally. The treatment is repeated in two weeks.

Nematodes (Roundworms): Several effective treatments are available.

Levamisole, an injectible intraperitoneal treatment, should be administered at a dosage of 10 mg/kg and the treatment repeated in two weeks.

Ivermectin, injected intramuscularly in a dosage of 200 mcg/kg is effective. The treatment is to be repeated in two weeks. Ivermectin can be toxic to certain taxa.

Thiabendazole and **Fenbendazole** have similar dosages. Both are administered orally at 50–100 mg/kg. Fenbendazole is usually administered on three successive days, and then repeated in 14 days for three more days. Thiabendazole is repeated in 14 days.

Mebendazole is administered orally at a dosage of 20–25 mg/kg and repeated in 14 days.

Breeding

All members of both the Varanidae and the teiids are oviparous; they lay eggs.

Because of the low percentage of successful breedings (and even lower percentage of successful hatchings), we know that we have a lot to learn for long-term success with these lizards. Many clutches will go full term, yet the babies will fail to hatch, or of those that do hatch, some will be deformed. This would indicate improper relative humidity and/or temperatures during incubation. Thus, many of the reproductive parameters suggested in both this section and the species accounts are conjectural.

Although successful breeding of monitors and tegus in captivity often seems to be the "luck of the draw," there are a few things you can do to stack the deck in your favor:
• retaining your specimens in A-1 health—not skinny, not obese, no endoparasites
• caging suitable (from *all* husbandry aspects) but especially temperature regime, space, humidity, and lighting
• accurate sexing of your monitors and tegus (not always easy)
• manipulating photoperiods (natural seems best)
• simulating variation in seasonal temperatures or humidity and rainfall
• cycling your specimens
• introducing a second male to stimulate agonistic (territorial/aggressive) behavior, which, after dominance is determined, will often turn to reproductive activity

Important: Do not get discouraged if, after all of your efforts, your lizards fail to breed. Even those monitors and tegus known to be compatible, proven breeders may fail some years. This is especially so if they are moved from familiar caging or if disturbing alterations are made to existing caging.

Of the comparatively few monitor breedings reported in the United States, most success has been had with monitors maintained year round in quasi-natural outside facilities. Such caging and maintenance programs are possible in southern Florida, Texas' Lower Rio Grande Valley, and some areas of Arizona and southern California. In cooler areas, with protection and forethought (and southern exposures), monitors and tegus can be maintained outside seasonally. If maintained indoors, it will be necessary to fulfill all of the parameters already mentioned *and* to provide sufficient full-spectrum lighting to induce natural behavior. This is not an easy task. Despite our best efforts to provide the artificial illumination necessary for monitors and tegus maintained indoors, there really is no substitute for natural unfiltered sunlight to stimulate natural (including reproductive) behavior.

Specifics for inducing breeding in monitors and tegus, when known, will be mentioned in the individual species accounts. Many of the monitor breeding parameters mentioned in the species accounts are based on, and extrapolated from, successes with specimens kept in outside facilities. For some monitors, there are no captive breeding accounts, either inside or out, on which we may rely.

Hatchling monitors of some species are more brightly colored or strongly patterned than the adults. This is a freshly hatched white-throated monitor, Varanus albigularis *ssp.*

Health

Unless they are healthy and relatively content, it is unlikely that your monitors will even attempt to breed, or if they do breed, that their efforts will be successful.

What equates to health and contentment in a monitor? As for any captive lizard, the most insidious and pervasive problem is stress. Stress, which we will define here as "unease," can be physical or psychological. Injury, ill health, incompatibility with other lizards, being too exposed, being too constrained, being too humid, or too arid—or anything else to excess—can cause stress. Serious stress may have an almost instantaneous adverse result, or the result may be as subtle as the stress itself. But it is a very real threat to the overall health of your lizard long-term. Stress may manifest itself as a loss of appetite, a continuing flight response, aggressive actions and reactions, cowering, or any other unnatural behavior by your lizard. The cause must be corrected. The correction may be as easy as providing a new or better hiding area, increasing or reducing heat, providing a more suitable basking area, removing a cagemate or placing an opaque barrier between monitor cages, moving the entire cage to a less heavily trafficked area, or altering the relative humidity or lighting. The cause may be complex and truly tax your ingenuity to determine its origin. Remember always that a stressed monitor cannot be a healthy or content monitor, nor can it correct the problem itself. The solution rests with you.

There are three important and easily assessed aspects of good health:
• suitable weight: neither thin nor obese, but just a little heavy is better than underweight
• freedom from endoparasites
• no respiratory distress

There are, of course, other physical criteria, less overt and more difficult to diagnose, with which time and experience will familiarize you.

Because the reproductive cycling of monitors usually involves cooling the lizards for a variable period of time, a full or partial fast during the period of cooling, and other things (discussed later) that can add an already stressful situation or further complicate existing health problems, we suggest that you not even try to cycle a monitor with known health problems. It is much better to correct the situation and wait for a year than to further compromise the well-being of the lizard. This is especially true if a respiratory or other potentially communicable health problem exists with a potential breeder. Allowing a sick monitor to come in contact with a healthy mate is irresponsible.

Sexing

Monitors are among the more difficult lizards to accurately sex by utilizing external differences. The males of some species are larger and bulkier than the females and have proportionately larger heads. But these differences are *proportional* and often very subtle. A heavily gravid female may actually be considerably heavier than a

40

similarly sized male. When near full term, an egg-laden female may show the lumpy outline of her eggs. Although sexual color differences are unusual among monitors, adult male Merten's water monitors often have the sides of their faces suffused with blue while those of the females are orange-yellow. Males also have bulges at the base of the tail, and the males of some have patches of modified scales at the tail base.

Of all sizes, it is the hatchlings of most species that are the most easily sexed. The hemipenes of hatchling males may be carefully and gently everted by utilizing the same "pressure and thumb-rolling" method breeders use to sex hatchling snakes. In this method the lizard is held upside down in one hand. The thumb of your other hand is placed subcaudally a few millimeters posterior to the lizard's vent, pressed firmly downward and rolled gently forward (towards the vent). The pressure will cause the hemipenes of the male to evert. Females, of course, lack hemipenes, but will have a small reddish dot on the tissue on each side of the vent. Done improperly, this technique can injure your lizard. We strongly urge that you utilize the services of an experienced herpetoculturist until you are fully comfortable and adept with the procedure. "Probing," again similar to that done to sex snakes, can also be used. Probing, too, must be done very carefully (seek experienced help) and is not 100 percent accurate, even when done by experts.

There are times when, if you are observant, the lizard may inform you of its sex. Males, both young and old, may voluntarily evert or protrude their hemipenes if disturbed. They may do this occasionally while just foraging in their cage, but are most prone to resorting to hemipenial eversion if they are grasped, immobilized and turned

A female Merten's water monitor (V. mertensi) in breeding readiness will have gold rather than blue lips.

upside down. Be careful when doing this! The method often causes the frightened lizard to void its intestinal content as well. If hemipenial eversion does occur, you will, of course, be certain that the lizard is a male. But if this doesn't occur, you will not necessarily know for certain whether the specimen is a male that merely didn't choose to evert its hemipenis or a female that had none to evert.

Radiographing, occasionally done at zoos, can accurately sex monitors by showing the presence or lack of a pair of hemipenile bones, one on each side of and just posterior to the anal opening. Males have these bone spurs; females lack them. But radiography exposes the gonads to unnecessary radiation.

HOW-TO:
Making Your Own Incubator

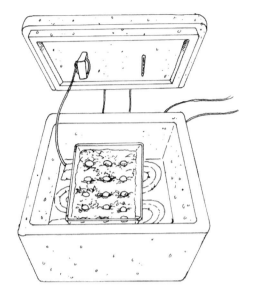

Homemade incubator.

Materials needed for one incubator:

1 wafer thermostat (obtainable from feed stores; these are commonly used in incubators for chicks)

1 heat tape, available from gardening stores or hardware stores

1 thermometer

1 Styrofoam cooler—one with thick sides (a fish shipping box is ideal)

Enough ½ × 2 inch (1.3 × 5 cm) mesh hardware cloth to bend into a "u" shape to hold the egg containers above the heat tape

Poke a hole through the lid of the cooler and suspend the thermostat from the inside. The L-pin "handle" on the top of the thermostat is the rheostat, and you'll use that to adjust the temperature. Add another hole through the lid for the thermometer, so you can check on the inside temperature without opening the top. If there's no flange on the thermometer to keep it from slipping through the hole in the lid, use a rubber band wound several times around the thermometer to form a flange.

Poke another hole through the lower side of the cooler and pull the heat tape through the hole. Arrange the tape in a continuous series of loops across the bottom of the cooler, and use wire nuts or electrician's tape to wire the heat tape to the thermostat. Put the lid on the cooler and plug in the thermostat/heater. Wait half an hour and check the temperature. Adjust the thermostat/heater until the temperature inside the incubator is about 80 to 86°F

(27–30°C). (See the species accounts so you'll know what temperature to use).

Once you have the temperature regulated, add your hardware cloth "shelf" and put the container of eggs atop the shelf. Close the lid.

Check the temperature daily and add a little water to the incubating medium as needed. The preferred humidity is 100 percent, which can be accomplished by keeping the hatching medium of peat and soil damp to the touch but too dry to squeeze out any water by your hand.

Let's Talk Temperature

What temperatures do we suggest for monitor husbandry? Let's look at a few examples. The following comments merely give some general ideas. Please check the various species accounts for additional comments. Note that the recommended temperatures for forest species of a given latitude vary less than those suggested for desert forms from the same latitude. This is simply because where tropical and subtropical temperatures are buffered by the forests, the day/night and season changes are usually noticeably less than in open deserts.

For how long should the period of cooling be maintained? The truth is that in most cases *no one* really knows. Since so very little is known with certainty about the reproductive biology of most monitors, many of the suggestions contained in this section are extrapolations from what is known about better understood lizards and snakes that dwell amongst the varanids.

With many of these other reptiles, the needed period of cooling varies from 30 to 75 days. It seems logical that a similar duration would be necessary for monitors, but experimentation is needed. Until known otherwise, we suggest that the winter regimen be maintained for a period of from 30 to 50 days.

Above all, keep records and disseminate knowledge. There are virtually no experts when it comes to monitor breeding techniques; only some folks who have been more or less consistently luckier than others.

Does your monitor require a period of dormancy to cycle reproductively? *Probably* not. Would it hurt to provide your monitor with a period of dormancy? Again, probably not, especially if it is a species that normally encounters cool to cold winter temperatures in the wild. And a short period of dormancy *might* do some good.

Monitors from southern subtropical latitudes (southernmost Australia and Africa) undergo periodic dormancy. The times of quietude may be restricted to an occasional few days during the passage of a cold front or may be of longer duration in areas that are normally cool to cold. These lizards may also estivate for variable durations during periods of extreme heat or drought.

The problem, of course, is that once a monitor of any species enters the general pet trade, it is impossible to know from what latitude it originated. Occasionally specialty dealers can give you some idea of the origin of a specimen that they are offering, or, if the species in question comes from circumscribed range, you can fairly well narrow its origin, hence its climatic requirements. But if it's a widely

Forest Species

Summer Highs		Basking Spot	Winter Lows		Basking Spot
Day	84–88°F (29–31°C)	87–90°F (30–32°C)	Day	80–84°F (27–29°C)	84–88°F (29–31°C)
Night	76–80°F (24–27°C)	off	Night	68–72°F (20–22°C)	off

Desert Species

Day	86–92°F (30–33°C)	90–98°F (32–37°C)	Day	72–76°F (22–24°C)	80–84°F (27–29°C)
Night	75–80°F (24–27°C)	off	Night	65–70°F (18–21°C)	off

Although monitors are bred with increasing regularity, success is still noteworthy. Merten's water monitors hatching at Glades Herp, Inc.

active before and during a severe thunderstorm, the passage of a frontal system, or a tropical depression. The activity of the lizards is caused by the lowering of the barometric pressure associated with such weather patterns. Utilize and enhance these periods of naturally increased activity by misting, warming, cooling, adding a second male, or doing whatever else may enhance the possibility of sexual interest.

The male dominance factor (protecting of territory from incursions by other males) is known to be an important aspect of the life histories of most lizard species. Natural dominance behavior has been well documented in populations of many varanids and teiids.

Inducing male dominance can be an important tool to the breeder of varanids. Interactions between males can be stressful to both of the participants and, if not carefully supervised by the keeper, can actually prove fatal in the "worst case scenario."

However if worked to best advantage, it may sufficiently sexually stimulate *both* males that both will repeatedly and successfully breed the females.

ranging species like the savanna or the Nile monitor, the best you can ever do is guess. In most cases, the combination of parameters that we have suggested—the reduction of photoperiod, temperature, humidity, and feeding frequency—will probably be sufficient to stimulate reproductive cycling.

Whether your animals are maintained indoors or outdoors, learn to make the most of changes in barometric pressure. You will note that even those specimens kept indoors, under conditions that are entirely artificial, in cages where they are unable to see the outdoors, become more

Breeding Your Tegus (and relatives)

It is not without justification that the macroteiids are often spoken of as the "ecological equivalents of the monitors." Though there are no true "giants" among the teiids, the members of these two dissimilar but convergent groups (monitors and tegus) are of similar appearance, habits, and, for the most part, ecology.

As captives, the members of the two groups require much the same care, from spacious cages to health and stress controls. Please note that both the red and the black and white tegus seem to require a lengthy period of complete dormancy. Both species

Like the black and white tegu, the red tegu, T. rufescens, *requires a lengthy period of hibernation to cycle reproductively.*

cease feeding and begin preparing for dormancy while the weather is still quite warm. It will be necessary for you to consider this when breeding preparations are being made. Tegus are unusual in that they actually build a nest suitable for egg deposition, another factor which you will need to consider and provide for.

Because there are so few species of tegus, the factors pertinent to the breeding of these teiid lizards (when known) are included in detail in the various species accounts. The reproductive biology of the two "dwarf tegus," *Callopistes* species and the two caiman lizards, *Dracaena* species, remains largely unknown. It is only three tegus of the genus *Tupinambis* that are bred with any regularity, and this only recently. Those tegus bred with most success are the most southerly two, the black and white, *T. merianae* and the red, *T. rufescens.* In both cases, the big lizards are being bred outdoors, and extrapolation from those conditions will be necessary if you wish to succeed in indoor facilities.

Nesting Facilities: Both tegus and monitors bury their eggs, often deeply, in suitably warmed and moistened substrate. Large monitors dig nests about 30 inches (75 cm) in depth, and small species may dig nests only a few inches (to 10 cm) deep. In most cases, at least in captivity, the preferred medium seems to be earth, either brought into their indoor cages or occurring naturally in outside facilities. In some cases deepened substrate has been provided in nesting boxes. Unsuitably heated and moist-

Nesting area for tegu.

ened substrate may induce the female monitor to retain eggs beyond their normal developmental duration. Ground surface temperatures of from 85°F (29°C) to close to 100°F (37.7°C) have been reported at the nesting sites of various monitors. The ground surface temperatures of many desert species are often understandably higher than those recorded for woodland/forest species. In all cases, at the time measured, the actual nest temperature was considerably cooler—76°F (24°C) to about 82°F (28°C).

In all cases, the eggs were removed from the nests and incubated artificially. As mentioned, success has varied, and additional knowledge and experimentation is needed from both the professional and amateur herpetoculturists who choose to work with these magnificent lizards.

Taxonomy—A Far from Final Word on Names

As you browse our text, you will note comments about the uncertainty of names applied here, or elsewhere, to the described species. The uncertainty involves not only the common names, but scientific names as well. The discrepancies exist because the very concept of evolutionary biology—the concept on which our present system of nomenclature is based—is currently being reassessed.

Many contemporary taxonomists no longer recognize subspecies. To others there may be philosophical differences in species, generic, or even familial concepts. It is not our intent to argue any point here, but since we are most comfortable with evolutionary concepts, it is those names that we have used (and even then we have been conservative). In all cases, when a given species is referred to by more than a single name, we have tried to cross-reference the fact. We urge you to check the species accounts and the index before becoming discouraged. Additional changes will undoubtedly occur. However, for now, these names used herein seem most prudent, and, whether agreed with or not, are understandable by both herpetologists and herpetoculturists.

Photography

Photography, in a way, is a great equalizer. Although many hobbyists worldwide keep monitors and tegus, few have a chance to see these lizards in the wild. Photos have enabled all enthusiasts to "see" the animals, albeit vicariously. In recent years, with the expansion of the business of ecotourism, more individuals have been able to see the animals for themselves. Now some firms, such as Green Tracks, Inc. (Tyler, Texas), specialize in reptile and amphibian sighting-and-photography trips. Green Tracks regularly guides small groups to the Amazon Basin, where tegus are abundant and caiman lizards can be occasionally found, and are expanding the scope of their tours to include southern Africa. There participants may encounter monitors in the wild.

If you need to stay closer to home, zoos now offer naturalistic displays of monitors from the size of the Komodo dragon on down. We urge all of you to record your visits to the world's wild places, and even to zoological gardens, on film. With today's proliferation of film types, from instant photos to videos to prints to slides, choosing a format may be a challenge. We like to make our photographic records on slides. When these are projected, a roomful of enthusiasts can vicariously enjoy the scenery and the lizards. An ever-increasing number of travelers prefer videos. These are ideal for home appreciation.

Whether you use videos, slides, or prints, keep photographic records and include dates and locations.

Still photography of lizards, meaning the subject is not moving and is quite literally "still," can be a truly enjoyable challenge. "Capturing" lizards on film at home or in the wild requires discipline, skill, a little knowledge, and a lot of luck. When developed, each photo helps you to see how the next could be improved.

The equipment required depends upon a number of variables. Among these are whether you will be taking photos of large lizards or small lizards, whether the photos will be of captives, staged, or in the wild, and whether or not you are willing to devote to the hobby the time necessary to be successful. Photographing captive or staged lizards is of course infinitely easier than pursuing and photographing free-ranging ones, but not nearly as satisfying.

Basic Equipment Needs

A sturdy 35-mm camera body with interchangeable lenses is suggested. You don't need a new camera body and lenses; we've used quality

When trying field photography, approach the lizard slowly and avoid eye contact.

47

A variety of photo equipment.

secondhand equipment for many of our photographic ventures. You do need a photo supply dealer who can advise about the condition of the equipment you're buying and who can tell you about that particular lens or body; secondhand camera equipment only rarely comes with manuals, and if you're like us, guesswork is not wholly successful.

The lenses we use

28-mm wide-angle for habitat photos

50-mm standard for habitat photos

100-mm macro for close-ups (suitable for almost every purpose)

75 to 205-mm zoom lens for variable fieldwork

400-mm fixed focal length telephoto lens for fieldwork

120 to 600 zoom lens for distant but variable fieldwork

Strobes: A series of dedicated strobes (a dedicated strobe interfaces with the camera f-stop setting to furnish appropriate light levels)

Lens adapter: a ×1.25 to ×2 power lens adapter (doubler).

Film

ISO 50 slide film is slower, hence less "grainy" than the faster films often used for other purposes. This slower film will give you the best results, but also requires a bright day or electronic flashes to compensate for the slow speed. The higher the ISO, the less light you will need to photograph, but the "grainier" your pictures will be. If you are taking pictures with the hope of having them published, use ISO 50 slide film. If you are taking photos merely for your own enjoyment, use either slide or print film, as you prefer.

Tripod

A sturdy tripod (an absolute necessity for the telephoto lenses) will hold your camera steady while you squeeze off that "once-in-a-lifetime" shot. Camera equipment with lenses is heavy, especially if you're out in the field and have slogged through hip-deep water and then scaled a couple of hillsides. The equipment is heavy even if you're indoors. Having a strong assistant along helps.

Camera body

After having a camera body malfunction on occasion, we now always have at least one spare body available.

Some Photographic Hints

For staged photography, create a small suitably natural setting by using a sand or leaf substrate with additional props of rocks or limbs—whatever is most appropriate for the species you're photographing. In the past, we used a small lazy Susan as a stage, thinking that for different photographic angles we could rotate the stage with the animal on it. This works, providing that you move very slowly, both in your own actions and in rotating the stage. If you don't have a lazy Susan, just arrange the setting items on a table or on a tree stump (outdoors or in, depending on where you are at the time), place the lizard, focus, and shoot. Having another person stand-

Opportunities for field photography of reptiles are now being provided by ecotourism specialists. Pictured is a desert Gould's monitor, V. g. flavirufus.

ing by to catch the lizard when it decides to scoot off (as it almost invariably will do) will help.

Generally, if you don't spook the lizard, it will pause long enough in place to permit you to get a few shots. You'll need to move quickly to capture either monitors or tegus when they dart away just before you've gotten that one truly good shot that you've been striving for. These lizards are fast!

We created a backing for our stage with the top half of a round trash can, sectioned to size and then bolted into place just inside the edge rim of the lazy Susan. Black velvet clipped into place around the inside surface of the background enhances the setting.

If you're trying field photography, approach the animal slowly and obliquely. Avoid eye contact. If the lizard notices you (of course it will!) freeze for a moment, then begin moving again. In some cases, you may need to approach as closely as possible in a vehicle. We've taken many

Lazy Susan stage with lizard.

photos in this manner, not because of comfort (although there are places where this certainly would count!), but because many lizards will allow a closer approach.

In photography, if practice does not make perfect, it at least makes better. Enjoy!

Introduction to the Monitors

The Lizard Family Varanidae

The ranks of the monitors include the world's largest as well as some of the world's smallest lizard species. All are protected by international conservation treaties, and many by specific laws of the various countries to which they are indigenous.

Of Asian, African, Australian, and Indonesian distribution, the monitor lizards range in size from the heavy-bodied ten feet (3 m) attained by males of the Indonesian Komodo monitor, *Varanus komodoensis* (also called "dragon lizard"), down to the barely eight-inch (20 cm) overall length of the Australian short-tailed monitor, *V. brevicauda*. Between these extremes are some 25 to 30 additional species of more moderate lengths.

A few halfhearted attempts have been made to elevate the subgeneric names of the monitors to full generic names. Thus, in some publications you may see monitors referred to by genera such as *Odatria, Tectovaranus, Indovaranus, Empagusia, Psammosaurus,* and others. These designations may be written in one of several ways: *Varanus (Empagusia) exanthematicus, V. (Empagusia) exanthematicus, Varanus (E.) exanthematicus*. Although these divisions are rather generally accepted as valid subgenera, immediate resistance to their elevation above that level was felt. Thus, all monitors continue to be in the genus *Varanus*, and it is as such that we refer to them here.

Monitors are thought to be the most snakelike of the lizards, with greatly protrusible tongues and well developed Jacobson's organs. The Jacobson's organs, located on the roof of the mouth, analyze the chemosensory data transferred by the tongue.

All monitors have well-developed eyelids and easily discernible ear openings.

All have a more or less attenuate form (with the African savanna and white-throated monitors proportionately the heaviest at all stages of their lives and the adults of the Komodo dragon especially robust).

All have strong, well-developed legs with five toes on each foot.

Although it may be exceeded in length by the crocodile monitor, no other monitor equals the Komodo dragon, V. komodoensis, *in body bulk.*

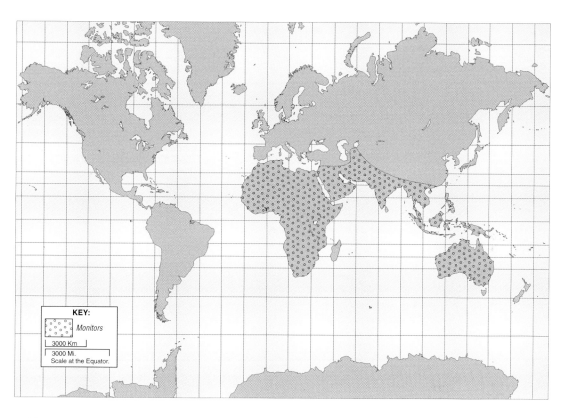

The claws can be recurved and needle-sharp to assist with climbing, sharp but less recurved (rock-dwelling species), or considerably blunter and of little use in climbing (certain terrestrial forms).

Monitors' tails lack fracture planes and are nonregenerable.

All monitors are oviparous.

Although monitors are not capable of any great degree of color change, cool specimens are often somewhat darker than warm ones. The darker hues facilitate rapid warming (thermoregulation) while the lighter ones better reflect heat, thus helping to prevent a critical overwarming.

Monitors are all highly predatory, consuming, according to their sizes and abilities, insects, fish, amphibians,

Monitor climbing, showing attenuate form, protrusible tongue, eyelids, ear opening, strong legs and claws.

Monitor reacting nastily after sunning.

There are now some nine monitor species regularly available to the pet trade and at least three more that are sporadically seen. Only two are in the low-to-moderate price range. These are the African savanna monitor and the African Nile monitor. Other more expensive species that are occasionally seen are the white-throated monitor, of African origin, the Asian water monitor, the mangrove monitor (including the beautiful blue-tailed morph) and two Indonesian tree monitors, the green and the black. Of the smaller semiarboreal species, the Timor is often available, and of the terrestrial/saxicolous monitors, the Australian ridge-tailed is now the monitor most frequently offered.

other reptiles, eggs, rodents, birds, hares, and in the case of the gigantic Komodo monitor, goats, deer, and similarly sized animals. Nor do food items need to be alive, or even fresh.

The long, protrusible, forked tongues of monitors carry scents to sensory organs in the lizard's mouth. Pictured is a southern argus monitor, V. panoptes rubidus, *in New South Wales, Australia.*

The savanna monitor (top) remains inexpensive and readily available in the pet trade. The mangrove monitor (bottom) is more expensive and less readily available.

Some Pet Store Favorites

African Monitors

Of the three most commonly seen African monitors, two are stocky land-lubbers that attain a length of about 5 feet (1.5 m), and the other is a more attenuated semiaquatic species that occasionally exceeds 7 feet (2 m) in length. The first two, the savanna and the white-throated monitors, were long thought to be conspecific. It has been demonstrated, however, that, although quite similar externally and closely related, the savanna and the white-throated monitors are sufficiently dis-similar to warrant their current taxonomic separation into two species. In older texts you will find white-throated monitors listed as a subspecies of the savanna.

It should also be noted that in some of its populations the common name of "white-throated monitor" applied to *Varanus albigularis* is clearly erroneous. Many specimens have off-white, dusky, or even black throats.

Savanna and white-throated moni-tors display a remarkable tolerance (immunity?) to the venom of many of the snake species that occur in the same habitat.

The Savanna Monitor, *Varanus exanthematicus*

[Savanna or Savanna*h*? It's all in the preference and the country! In the United States, a savanna(h) is defined as a treeless plain. Savannah is also a major city in the state of Georgia. We prefer to delete the final "h" when speaking of a geologic phenomenon and to use the "h" when speaking of the Georgia city.]

The African savanna monitor, *V. exanthematicus* is immensely popular in the pet trade. It is a grayish species with darker and lighter markings and much enlarged, roughened nuchal (nape) scales. The dorsal markings of juveniles often take the form of cross-bands of light-centered dark eyelike ocelli. The body color of all will be lighter and prettier when the lizards are suitably warm and unstressed.

The savanna monitor is a propor-tionately stocky, dry-land species. It commonly attains a length of about five feet (150 cm), and some speci-mens may near six (2 m). With advanced age, during times of plenty, savanna monitors can become grossly obese. It is probably no more healthy for a monitor to be decidedly over-weight than it is for a human to be so. Reasonable efforts should be made to keep the weight of captive savanna monitors within acceptable parame-ters. Unfortunately, there is no monitor size/weight chart yet produced. Your intuition will necessarily be your guide, but be aware—fat is not better, espe-cially if you are hoping for longevity records or breeding success.

Frightened specimens huff and puff and inflate their body and gular area alarmingly, turn sideways to the per-ceived threat, and lash with their tail. Tame specimens forego this and will often actually crawl onto their owner's lap. As this indicates, savanna monitors can become very tame. However—they are also *always* ready to eat. They quickly learn to associate the presence of a human with food. Be careful when initially reaching for them. A bite by a large specimen, intended or not, can be a painful ordeal!

Savanna, white-throated, and some other monitor species utilize an interesting ploy when confronted by a large predator. When severely frightened, the lizards will arc their body and grasp a hindlimb in the mouth. In this position they present a larger, and perhaps unappealing aspect, to the confronting predator. Similar defensive positioning is utilized by other distinctly different lizards, the armadillo lizard, *Cordylus cataphractus,* being the best known.

About breeding: Although monitors of many kinds are considered difficult to breed, both private hobbyists and zoological gardens have succeeded a few times with the savanna monitor. Because of the vast number of wild-collected babies currently being imported for the pet trade, the prices of savanna monitors are so deflated that no large-scale captive-breeding programs have yet been instituted. Thus it is only the most dedicated of hobbyists, those who wish to breed savanna monitors for research rather than monetary gain, who have pursued the reproductive biology of the species. Although it is encouraging that at least some are seriously working with this monitor, it is sad that more hobbyists are not. Although this is still a rather common species over much of its sub-Saharan range, no species can perpetually withstand the onslaught of the pet and skin trades. Someday the importations of this species will come to a screeching halt (as they have for other once commonly seen species) and we will then be dependent on the knowledge

The white-throated monitor (bottom) was once considered a subspecies of the savanna monitor (top).

gained from those who chose to learn before it was actually necessary to do so. Then their wisdom may begin to benefit them financially.

Male monitors are not only territorial, they are extremely defensive of their territories. This is especially true during the breeding season. Although they may wander widely, keen vision and an equally keen olfactory sense reliably inform monitors of interlopers. During the breeding season interlopers are quickly investigated, with males being challenged, females being bred,

Savanna monitors are stocky and often easily tamed. Cool specimens are often darker in coloration than warm ones.

and juveniles being ignored (if large but yet subadult) or eaten. Readers of natural history books or watchers of nature channels on TV may well be familiar with the territorial and breeding-related grapplings of the males of several species of Australian monitors. Each male raises its torso high from the ground, and while in a tripedal stance (supported by hind limbs and tail) grapples and rakes at the other with its foreclaws in an attempt to topple and dominate the opponent. In some instances, rear claws are

Healthy, acclimated savanna monitors will feed eagerly. A varied diet of insects and mice seems to be the best food.

employed as well. These interactions may well be important to successful breedings by many monitor species, the savanna among them; the drama may be nearly as important in captivity as in the wild.

In nature, it is usually the dominant male that "wins" the female. Dominance and territorialty certainly seem to figure prominently in the reproductive readiness of varanid lizards.

Clutches of as many as 50 eggs have been recorded, but most clutches are half that size, or fewer. A chamber dug into the side of a termitarium may occasionally be used, but apparently over much of its range the savanna monitor merely digs a hole in suitably moist, easily worked earth.

The White-Throated Monitor, *V. albigularis* ssp.

Like the savanna monitor, the white-throated monitor is a very heavy-bodied, terrestrial species. Some become tame if acquired when young and worked with diligently, but most seem less tractable than savanna monitors treated similarly. In fact, even with considerable attention, many white-throated monitors remain quite irascible. Handling an unruly adult can be a painful proposition.

Despite comments by other authors to the contrary, some specimens of the white-throated and the savanna monitors can be quite difficult to differentiate—especially for a new enthusiast. In general, white-throated monitors are darker and more strongly banded than savannas. The top of the head and the nape, between the nearly black temporal stripes (which may be well-defined or obscure and either converge or diverge on the posterior nape) are usually especially dark. The tail is prominently banded.

Although *V. albigularis* had long been referred to as a separate species by both hobbyists and herpetoculturists, it was only in 1989 that the savanna and white-throated monitors were *officially* (scientifically) separated. Long overdue research dictated the change. In that year, the official name of the newly elevated species became *Varanus albigularis,* and it, itself, was quickly separated into a number of questionable subspecies. Besides the nominate form, there are *V. a. microstictus* (questionably valid) and *V. a. ionidesi* (now invalid but the designation is still used by pet dealers). In 1989 *V. yemenesis* was described. Since then its validity has been questioned by some taxonomists and accepted by others. The characteristics used to separate this big lizard from *V. albigularis,* obviously its closest relative, will probably be bandied around for years. Only time will tell whether the Yemen monitor will be accepted by the scientific community as a fully distinct species.

The babies of the white-throated monitor are strikingly marked. Hatchlings have a dark head that, with growth, becomes progressively darker. The dark temporal and nuchal stripes are particularly well developed on the young. These may be retained by adults, but the progressive suffusing of the head and shoulders with dark pigment often obliterates the markings.

Attaining somewhat more than 6 feet (2 m), Tanzanian white-throats (with black throats!) were once considered the subspecies, *V. a. ionidesi.* They were popularly referred to as Ionides' monitors. Although the subspecific status is no longer recognized, these do seem to be distinctively patterned and colored lizards.

Rob MacInnes and Bill Love of Glades Herp in Ft. Myers, Florida may have been the first persons in the continental United States to have bred the Tanzanian white-throated monitor in captivity. We were present when the breeders, adult imports from Tanzania,

The reddish color of this newly imported white-throated monitor is caused by iron or other soil components. The normal black and white color can be seen where the skin has been shed.

were unpacked from their shipping crate. We remember thinking them to be little more than gaping, tooth-studded jaws, sharp claws, and whipping tail. Wild-collected monitors—especially *large* wild-collected monitors—of most species are adept at presenting this appearance, and with monitors at least, appearances do not lie! Large wild specimens can be difficult, even *dangerous*, to handle.

The adults were taken to a 10-foot by 10-foot (3 m × 3 m) cage in a screened greenhouse, where they still reside.

This black-throated phase of the white-throated monitor was once designated V. albigularis ionidesi. *This is no longer a recognized subspecies.*

It took several years of acclimatizing in this quasi-natural setting (with natural sunlight and photoperiods) for the lizards to feel enough at home to successfully breed. The clutch numbered ten good eggs and two infertile masses. The female laid the clutch on the bare plywood floor of a 4 × 8 foot (1.2 × 2.5 m) hiding box after diligently scraping all of the mulch *away*. The first hatchling emerged after 150 days of incubation at 84°F (28.8°C).

In the wild, clutches of up to 37 eggs have been found. Deposition sites vary. Some females seem to prefer digging their nests into the almost cement-hard termitaria that dot their habitats. In an effort to retain the humidity so necessary to their existence, the insects soon reconstruct the mound, thus protecting the monitor eggs now contained within. In other cases, the nest is merely dug in moisture-retaining damp earth. When subjected to the vagaries of natural incubation, it may take the eggs in some nests nearly a year to hatch.

Although the two are now considered separate species, most of what has been said about the savanna monitor applies equally to the white-throat.

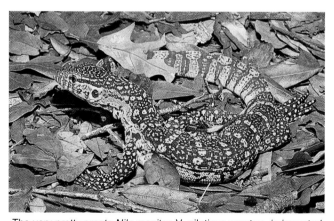

The very pretty ornate Nile monitor, V. niloticus ornatus, *is imported from the African country of Burundi.*

The Nile Monitor, *V. niloticus* ssp.

Despite its typically bad disposition (which may or may not modify favorably with handling), the Nile monitor is a common pet trade species, both in Europe and America. As a baby, sitting quietly or moving slinkily through its cage, the Nile is an engaging little creature. However, most Nile monitors do not tame sufficiently to make particularly good pets (a fact that the vendors often fail to mention). Although advancing age and frequent gentle handling may quiet them somewhat, seldom do Nile monitors make as tractable a pet as many other monitor species. Despite their ready availability, we don't recommend this species to any but the most dedicated and experienced of hobbyists.

The color of the Nile monitor, *V. niloticus,* is blackish with varying numbers of yellow spots forming cross-bands. Based on color and pattern, European researchers recognize more than a half dozen subspecies. At present, only two (*niloticus* and *ornatus*) are recognized by American taxonomists. *Ornatus* is a particularly pretty form. On it the large rounded yellow spots are contained in broad, otherwise unmarked, black bands. These contrast strongly with the buffered black of the rest of the body. The yellow spots lengthen into short cross-bars posteriorly and are complete bands on the tail. The *niloticus* form is more variable, but the yellow spots or bands are not contained within a contrasting black band. Between the yellow, the body may vary from solid black to black well buffered (lightened) with the tiniest of yellowish pepperings. The limbs are usually well marked with prominent discrete spots, but may be finely peppered with yellow in some phases. From one to four U-shaped yellow markings are usually present on the rear of the head and the nape.

The ornate Nile monitor is thought to be restricted to forested areas and their immediate environs in western Africa. The nominate race may be encountered over a wide variety of riverine, lakeside, or floodplain habitats from Egypt to extreme southeastern South Africa.

When walking, the Nile monitor holds its body high from the substrate on powerful legs, while the long motile tongue busily probes every nook and cranny, searching for prey or an avenue of escape, should the latter become necessary.

If larger than a hatchling when collected, there is probably no species of monitor harder to tame.

If frightened or engaged in territorial behavior, Nile monitors indulge in impressive and effective defense and threat postures. The body is inflated with air, but compressed vertically. The monitor stands high on its legs, hisses, whips the tail, and bites if the opportunity occurs. Monitors of all ages display in this manner.

In the wild, female Nile monitors show a decided preference for nesting in the termitaria that are found in their habitats. Within the termite mound, a steady temperature and high humidity is retained. The fact that the female monitors are able to dig through the mounds' sun-baked outer shell—barricades legendarily of almost cementlike hardness—is mute testimony to the effectiveness of the sharp claws and the strength of the lizard's legs. Since egg deposition often takes place during the time of summer rains, the termite mound may be softened somewhat, but they are still anything but soft. In some cases the completion of the nest may take the female monitor several days. After egg deposition has been completed, the termites repair their mound. The closure again retains temperatures and humidity ideal for the development of the monitor eggs.

Nile monitors, even when acquired as hatchlings, can be difficult to tame. This is a hatchling V. n. niloticus.

In captivity, female Nile monitors will dig a deep nesting chamber in moist (*not* wet) earth. They may more readily do so if the earth is contained in a barrel or is secluded behind some sort of opaque barrier. The female will have to be comfortable and unstressed to nest. Unless conditions are conducive to nesting, the female Nile monitor may just scatter her eggs

Although babies are agile climbers, with growth, Nile monitors become less arboreal and more aquatic.

on the floor of her cage or, worse yet, retain them until egg solidification or adherence occurs, both of which require surgical intervention.

Nile monitors lay large clutches. More than 15 eggs are normally laid, and clutches of over 50 eggs have been recorded.

In nature, the eggs may take the better part of a year to incubate, the hatchlings emerging from their termite mound cavity when the summer rains again soften the exterior somewhat. Incubation in captivity may take somewhat less than half that expected in the wild.

If fed adequately and kept suitably warm, hatchlings will grow quickly. A sizable water container—one large enough for the lizard to climb in and submerge—should be provided for this species.

Although most adults are smaller, Nile monitors can attain a length of more than 6.5 feet (2 m). The babies, which are quite arboreal, are opportunistic feeders on insects and other arthropods, carrion, smaller lizards, nestling rodents, or whatever else they can ferret out. They use both visual and chemical cues when hunting. Their long snout serves them in good stead, allowing them to grasp insects in narrow spaces. With growth, many changes occur in the Nile monitor. In answer to a changing diet, the skull becomes heavier and the snout less attenuate. This allows the lizard to

V. griseus, *an endangered species.*

easily overpower the mollusk, crustacean, fish, and mammalian components of the diet that it now utilizes. The Nile monitor's fondness for the eggs of crocodiles is well documented and often stated. With increased size, the Nile monitor becomes less arboreal, returning instead to terrestrial and aquatic habitats. It is a powerful swimmer that may be seen some distance from land.

Asian/Indonesian Monitors

There are no longer any monitors from elsewhere in the world that sell as inexpensively in the United States as the African species. Nowadays, even the once commonly imported Asian water monitor, *V. salvator* ssp., command prices of more than $100. Nor are any of the Asian monitors as readily available in the pet trade as the three African species already discussed.

Dumeril's Monitor, *V. dumerilii* ssp. and Rough-Necked Monitor, *V. rudicollis*

The Malaysian Dumeril's monitor, *V. dumerilii* ssp., is spectacular as a hatchling and reasonably attractive as an adult. Hatchlings have fire-orange heads and yellow crossbars on a black body. With growth the head color and yellow of the bands all too quickly fade to olive-tan or olive-gray and the black lightens to olive-brown. Once acclimated, Dumeril's monitors are quiet and easily cared for. They attain a length of somewhat more than 5 feet (1.5 m) and are sporadically available in the pet trades of both America and Europe. The nuchal (nape) scales of most specimens seen in the pet trade are prominently enlarged but flattened, producing a tiled, rather than a roughened, tuberculate effect. The large scales continue down the lizard's back. The nuchal scales of Borneo specimens (seldom seen in the pet trade) tend to be more keeled. The dorsal scales of the Bornean Dumeril's are smaller than the nuchal scales. Adults of Dumeril's monitor are often mistaken for the rough-necked monitor, *V. rudicollis*, a species of similar size, but very *dissimilar* appearance, that often is imported in the same shipments. As a juvenile the rough-necked monitor lacks the orange head and yellow bars, having instead very thin light gray crossbars on a ground color of deep brown. The rough-necked monitor also has a very slender head and a particularly slender snout. The snout of the Dumeril's monitor is broad and rather flat—typically monitorlike. The larger, prominently projecting nape scales of *V. rudicollis* are also distinguishing. When the rough-necked monitor is viewed in profile, the individual points of the nape scale keels are readily seen.

The rough-necked monitor is a persistently arboreal species; Dumeril's is considerably less so, at least as an adult.

Like most other monitors, the vast majority of *V. dumerilii* in the pet trade of the world are wild-collected specimens.

Rarely, captive breedings have been reported. Clutches of from 4 to as many as 18 eggs have been mentioned. Because of the paucity of clutches, the optimum egg incubation temperature remains unknown. Temperatures as low as 82°F (28°C) have been suggested, and have apparently produced successful incubations. Certainly, a newly hatched clutch of babies of this species must be one of the most spectacular sights known to monitor keepers.

In the wild, Dumeril's monitors seem most abundant in littoral, estuarine, and riverine habitats. Adults are far more apt to take to the water than to the trees when startled. In keeping with this habit, captives should be pro-

Few lizards are more attractive than hatchling Dumeril's monitors, V. dumerilii.

vided with a large water receptacle preferably one sufficiently large for the lizard to clamber into, coil and submerge. Since many monitors defecate in their water containers, it may be necessary to completely clean and sterilize this at frequent intervals. Because of the frequency with which cleaning will be necessary, be certain that whatever receptacle you provide is easily handled.

Initially nervous, especially if of a larger size when trapped, if given a suitable hiding area and secure caging, a Dumeril's monitor will usually quiet down rather rapidly. Seldom

V. dumerilii.

Within weeks the orange fades and hatchling Dumeril's monitors (top) assume the color of the adults (bottom).

Crustaceans, mollusks, nestling birds, and small mammals seem to figure prominently in the diet of larger specimens. Insects, fish, and some carrion are also eaten, especially by smaller specimens.

Adult rough-necked monitors may exceed 4.5 feet (1.4 m) in total length. The fact that they are a slender, long-necked, long-legged lizard with an attenuated, semiprehensile tail (of about 60–65 percent, the overall length), causes them to look smaller than they actually are.

When startled, the rough-necked monitor usually tries to go upward. A vertically oriented cage will best serve its needs. A nervous monitor, a rough-neck will readily utilize elevated hide-boxes, and seems especially at home when tangles of branches and other such visual barriers are provided. It becomes even more secure when real or artificial vining plants are draped over the cagetop branches.

Like most monitors, *V. rudicollis* has been bred in captivity, but only infrequently, and more often by European than by American hobbyists. Suggested incubation temperature for 4 to 14 eggs is 82–84°F (28–29°C). At these temperatures, incubation takes about six months.

Although rough-necked monitors may not use a large soaking bowl as frequently as many other monitor species, they will, nonetheless, occasionally enjoy a long soak.

Freshly imported specimens of both the Dumeril's and rough-necked monitors can prove to be reluctant feeders. Dumeril's can usually be coaxed into accepting standard monitor fare—insects, small mice, high-quality canned reptile or cat foods, even some suitably sized fish. On the other hand, *V. rudicollis* can be a problematic holdout. Insects, small tree frogs, small lizards, and (occasionally) newborn mice might tempt them. We have

do specimens bite as frenziedly as other monitor species when restrained. They will, however, posture, hiss, and slap with their tail. Specimens that feel particularly threatened become semirigid and point their noses skyward, often closing their eyes as they do so. This posture is usually assumed by the subordinate specimen, either in the presence of a predator or in appeasement of another monitor.

had to force-feed some particularly debilitated specimens to get them started. We consider the rough-necked monitor a rather delicate and problematic captive.

The Emerald and the Black Tree Monitors, *V. prasinus* ssp. and *V. beccarii*

Of the several species commonly referred to in the pet trade as "tree monitors," only two Indonesian species, the emerald, *V. prasinus* and the black, *V. beccarii* are seen with any regularity. Although both are long, lithe, and prehensile-tailed, they are easily differentiated by color. The former has a leaf-green dorsum (occasionally considerably duller) across which usually run bands or spots of jet black (occasionally almost entirely lacking).

The aptly named black tree monitor is entirely black in coloration. Neither exceeds 34 inches (85 cm), of which somewhat more than 60 percent is slender, prehensile tail length. The tail prehensility is great enough to support the entire body weight of the monitor if necessary. The tail is usually loosely coiled when the monitor is at rest and wrapped loosely around a support when the lizard is active. The limbs are long and powerful, and the toes are tipped with sharp, recurved claws. The very long, sharp teeth and extremely powerful jaws of tree monitors are designed to quickly overpower the lizards, frogs, small mammals, and birds on which these species prey. We hasten to assure you that they are most effective on restraining fingers and hands as well.

The New Guinean emerald tree monitor, *V. prasinus,* is a species of the lower elevations of New Guinea and of some of the surrounding islands. Although emerald monitors seem less common far inland than in suitable habitats along the periphery of the island, this may be more a

An elongated "bird-like" snout and roughened nape scales identify the rough-necked monitor, V. rudicollis. *This species is often confused with the Dumeril's monitor.*

result of collectors' sampling techniques than of actuality. Certainly it is easier to collect along the coast than it is to penetrate deeply into the forests. Emeralds are one of the prettiest of all monitors. The lizards are coveted by private collectors and zoos alike. Most emerald monitors will prove quite hardy and will soon accept small mice as prey. However, a variety of prey is thought to be better for the lizards in the long run than mice

Although small and slender, the emerald tree monitor, V. prasinus, *can be a savage biter.*

When acquired, emerald tree monitors should be checked immediately for internal parasites.

alone. Crickets, grasshoppers, June beetles (easily collected around porch lights in the spring), king mealworms, and mice seem to be the most readily available prey. Some tree monitors will also accept an occasional strip of lean beef, good quality canned cat food, and monitor ration. Large slugs were especially relished by some tree monitors that we maintained. After eating one of these slimy creatures, the monitors would laboriously wipe the sides of their mouth against branches and leaves to remove the slug's viscid mucus. A daytime thermal gradient of from about 84–92°F (28.8–33°C) with a relative humidity of 75 percent or more is satisfactory. Nighttime temperatures can be a few degrees cooler—68–75°F (20–24°C) is a good range—and no "hot spot" or thermal gradient is necessary.

Because of their arboreal tendencies, emerald monitors should be housed in a tall cage and provided with a number of suitably sized limbs on which to climb. Secretive species, they fully utilize the hiding places provided by growing plants, securely affixed hollow limbs, or even cockatiel nesting boxes. When their cage habitat is being built, elevated basking limbs accessed by a diagonally affixed tree trunk should be also provided. Some keepers prefer flat plywood shelves to limbs, but we have found the plywood more difficult to keep clean and odorless. It is a good idea (although probably not mandatory) to provide an individual basking perch at about the same level for every emerald in a cage. This will often provide a degree of harmony not possible if the dominant specimen restricts access of subordinate specimens to a single desirable basking limb. A basking "hot spot"—95–98°F (35–36.6°C) should be provided on each perch. When multiple bulbs are used to provide several warmed basking areas, care must be taken that the cage does not become overheated.

Although reproductive success with this remarkable monitor remains the exception rather than the rule, the emerald monitor has now been bred by several zoos and by private hobbyists as well. More success has been experienced in Europe than in the United States. The reported clutches are small, numbering from as few as two eggs to five eggs.

At 86°F (30°C), the incubation takes slightly less than five months, and hatchlings vary from a reported 3½ inches (9 cm) to well over 5 inches (13 cm) in total length. If proper care is given, the growth of this monitor is rapid. A subadult size can be attained within the first year. It remains unknown at what age sexual maturity is attained, but it is probably not until two or even three years of age.

As is the case with many slender-bodied forest reptiles from habitats of high humidity, imported emerald and black tree monitors are often seriously dehydrated and stressed by the rigors of collection from the wild, followed by a variable period of holding, then shipping. It is imperative that a program of rehydration be begun immediately upon arrival (these species will usually respond well to a hydration chamber, pages 23 to 24). Stool samples or a cloacal wash should be taken and analyzed and an effective parasiticide given, if necessary.

Nearly everything stated about the emerald tree monitor applies equally to the black tree monitor. Even less is known about the reproductive biology of this species than is known about its green cousin. Clutch size seems the same, and preferred incubation temperatures are probably identical. This species has been bred in Europe, but we are unaware of successes by American hobbyists.

V. beccarii is another accomplished arborealist with a fully prehensile tail that is more than twice the SVL

Except for its coloration, the black tree monitor, V. beccarii, is very similar to the emerald tree monitor. This monitor does not like to be restrained or handled.

(snout-vent length). Often kept in a watchspring coil when the lizard is resting, the tail is usually held against a branch or loosely entwining it when the lizard is active.

Fecal examinations and any necessary treatment should be performed by a qualified veterinarian as quickly as possible after receiving the lizards. Since it often requires from two to six treatments to completely rid the lizard of endoparasites, veterinary assessment is important even if the monitor has received initial treatment when first imported. Like the emerald monitors, *V. beccarii* often become severely dehydrated during importation procedures. A program of rehydration (see section on hydration chamber, pages 23 to 24) should be immediately instituted. Once satisfactorily rehydrated, providing warmth—daytimes, 84–92°F (29–33°C) with a basking hot spot nearing 98°F (37°C)—and high cage humidity will do much to ensure successful acclimatization. During acclimatization, overall nighttime cage temperatures should be allowed to drop only *slightly*. The hot basking spot is not necessary at night. After complete stabilization, nighttime temperatures can be allowed to fall into the high 60s or low 70sF (19–23°C). At all times, both during and following stabilization, a feeling of seclusion and security, as well as high cage humidity, must be provided for black tree monitors.

As with the emerald monitor, the shy and active black tree monitor does best if provided with a large, vertically oriented cage. Firmly affixed hollow limbs, cockatiel nest boxes with easy access, or just tangles of crisscrossed branches placed well above floor level, and especially near the top of the cage, will be readily and habitually used.

If grasped carelessly, black tree monitors will readily bite, scratch, and void their cloacal contents. The teeth are long and very sharp, and they do not readily release their grip. The long legs and toes are powerful and the claws of needlelike sharpness. You will probably wish to release your hold on the lizard long before it chooses to release its hold on *you!*

The Mangrove Monitor, *V. indicus* ssp.

Once quite uncommon in the pet industry, mangrove monitors are now seen with some regularity in specialty shops and on reptile dealers' lists. Although even now far from inexpensive, these pretty, moderately sized monitors are available to hobbyists who are able to afford them.

V. indicus occurs along coastal North Australia and over most of the rest of the range of the species. Many of the specimens that enter the American pet trade are imported from the Solomon Islands. In coloration *V. indicus* is of a black (occasionally olive or olive-brown) ground color that is liberally peppered with small discrete yellow, cream, greenish, or white spots. The light spots are usually arranged in crossrows dorsally, but are more variably arranged laterally, where they are often more numerous. Thus, the lateral surfaces may appear somewhat lighter in color than the dorsum. Hatchlings and juveniles are more brilliantly colored than adults and some juveniles may bear secondary rows of pale blue spots between the yellow. The tail of juveniles is often vividly banded in black and white. Mangrove monitors may occasionally exceed 5 feet (1.5 m) in total length, but of this, most is tail.

If acquired young and handled often and gently, mangrove monitors of all phases tame fairly well. Large wild-collected specimens have formidable jaw power and sharp claws and can be a real chore to handle. To add insult to the injury they may cause, mangrove monitors are also able to slap smartly

A Watering Tip

Arboreal monitors (like many other arboreally oriented lizards) may not readily descend to the ground to drink from a pan. This is especially true of disoriented, newly imported lizards that, until capture, probably derived most (if not all) of their water requirements from water-filled treeholes and from lapping water flowing down limbs, trunks, and foliage during storms. For these lizards it is best to place a water receptacle on an elevated shelf near a favored basking or resting area. We have found that both the emerald and black tree monitors will readily drink from a water dish placed in the pot of an easily accessible hanging plant. They seem to notice, and be drawn to the plant, by the fresh droplets of water that remain on the leaves following mistings. It is very important that you place all water dishes where even the most seclusive of your lizards will most readily notice and drink from them. Improvise!

with their tail and as a last resort will void their often not inconsiderable cloacal contents on an unwary handler. However, even large specimens gentle with time and handling.

Mangrove monitors have mastered several media. They are admirable climbers, entirely at home in the water, and comfortable on land. However, if hard-pressed, they will usually take to the water if it is present, thus indicating their aquatic preferences. These monitors are often encountered in trees along fresh water billabongs but may be particularly common in mangrove-studded brackish and saltwater locations. This species has a wide range over much of southern Asia and northern Australia.

In keeping with their aquatic propensities, mangrove monitors feed on numerous creatures of their riparian and littoral habitats. Small specimens are adept at catching worms, snails, fish, crayfish, and the like. Some amount of carrion is also eaten, and if nestling rodents or birds of suitable size are encountered, it is unlikely that the monitor would pass them by. Larger specimens have been reported feeding on all of the above, as well as small turtles, snakes, and lizards. Captives will also accept lean raw meat. Robert Sprackland, who has kept this species for many years, has commented that the lizards seem to have problems digesting large mammalian prey. He suggests that mice, rather than rats, be offered to even large mangrove monitors.

As captives, mangrove monitors require spacious cages, hide-boxes, firmly affixed, elevated perches, and a sizable but easily cleaned water pan. Captives will spend hours (sometimes days) coiled in their water receptacles. They may remain submerged between breaths for the better part of an hour. This a warmth-loving monitor that seems to thrive at a cage temperature

Although widely distributed, most mangrove monitors, V. indicus, seen in the American pet trade are from the Solomon Islands.

Like many monitors, the mangrove is arboreal when young and more terrestrial and aquatic when an adult.

Once considered a subspecies of the mangrove monitor, the beautiful blue-tailed monitor is now scientifically designated V. doreanus.

Comments on the Blue-Tailed and the Peach-Throated Monitors

Both the blue-tailed and the peach-throated monitors have traditionally been sold by dealers as variants of the mangrove monitor as well as under several other names.

The blue-tailed monitor may be seen offered in the pet trade as *"V. indicus kalibecki"* or simply as *"V. kalibeck."* The scientific name *Varanus doreanus*, designated in 1994, but ignored until lately, seems more accurate.

The body color of the blue-tailed monitor is very similar to that of the mangrove monitor. However, the yellow dorsal dots of the blue-tailed monitor are larger. As indicated by its common name, the tail of this lizard is banded in black and *blue* (rather than in black and white). It is a very beautiful lizard that is much in demand by the pet industry. It attains only about 3.5 to 4 feet (2.7–3 m) in total length. The specimens in the pet trade of the world are probably collected in western Irian Jaya.

The true identity of the peach-throated monitor is equally problematic. This lizard was described in 1932 as a race of the mangrove monitor. Then called *Varanus indicus jobiensis,* it has since been referred to as *V. karlschmidti* (in error) and (with "indicus" removed) as *V. jobiensis.* This latter name may well be accurate and is gaining acceptance.

The peach-throated monitor is a pretty but quietly colored lizard. It does have a peach or orange throat, may have the vaguest blush of deepest blue on the distal portion of the tail, and is otherwise black, marked with the tiniest of yellow dots. The dots often coalesce into vague bands both dorsally and laterally. The head often lacks yellow speckling. The head conformation of this lizard seem more angular than on nominate *V. indicus.* The natural history of this uncommon New Guinean monitor remains enigmatic.

of 85–92°F (29–33°C). A basking area with a temperature of 96°F (35.5°C) will be used to thermoregulate, especially if the remainder of the cage is kept in the mid 80sF (29°C).

Like most other wild-collected monitors, fresh imports of the mangrove monitor can bear heavy loads of endoparasites. These should be identified and purged as quickly after receiving the specimen as possible.

The Irian Jayan peach-throated monitor is now identified as V. jobiensis. *It is only infrequently seen in the pet trade.*

We can find no reports of either the blue-tailed or the peach-throated monitors having been bred in captivity. Care for both should be similar to that provided the mangrove monitor.

The Asian Water Monitor, *V. salvator* ssp.

At first appearance, some hatchlings of the Asian water monitor are confusingly similar to babies of the African Nile monitor. When viewed critically, however, many differences will be seen. Perhaps the most diagnostic difference is the position of the nostril. This is about equidistant from the eye and the tip of the snout on Nile monitors, and close to the tip of the snout on Asian water monitors.

As juveniles, the hatchlings of the water monitor may be black, olive-black, or deep olive-brown. They may be either liberally or sparsely marked with bands and ocelli of yellow-ochre, bright yellow, or chalk-white. The light markings are more profuse on the sides than on the dorsum. Hatchlings and juveniles are more prominently patterned than adults. Adults of the water monitor tend to assume an olive-brown to deep brown ground coloration that is patterned with lighter crossbands and ocelli. The markings may vary from well-defined to obscure.

Currently, several subspecies of the water monitor are recognized by taxonomists. As with most other current taxonomic designations, not all subspecies are thought valid by all authorities. In truth, the entire group needs reassessment. The pet trade has contributed additional confusion by coining invalid names and name combinations. The most blatant of these latter, *V. salvator "komaini,"* is used by dealers for big, nearly entirely black "water" monitors that have been occasionally imported. The exact origin of these lizards seems unknown to the dealers, and while they are quite different in appearance from other water monitors, the applied scientific name is invalid. It is to be hoped that the taxonomic status of this form will soon be determined.

The widely flung Philippine Islands are home to several subspecies of *Varanus salvator.* One of the prettiest of these is the rather small *V. s. cumingi.* The babies are brilliantly patterned with orange dorsal and lateral spots, an orange head, and orange nape stripes against an olive-brown ground coloration. Although the colors fade with growth, even adult *cumingi* retain a degree of patterning unusual

The position of the nostril will help differentiate Asian water monitors from Nile monitors. The nostril is near the tip of the snout on the Asian water monitor (top) and nearer the eye on the Nile (bottom).

V. salvator.

in other races. At least two other less brightly colored races also occur on the Philippines. These are *V. s. marmoratus* and *V. s. nuchalis.* These two lizards seem marginally distinct from each other, being differentiated by the comparative size of the enlarged nape scales. None of the Philippine races of the water monitor is common in the pet trade. *V. s. togianus,* a dark, poorly known race from the Celebes, is even less frequently seen.

It is the nominate race, *V. s. salvator,* that is best known to both herpetologists and herpetoculturists and that has the widest range. This race occurs over much of Southeast Asia, on Irian Jaya, and on many Indonesian islands.

The name "water monitor" is not entirely accurate. The fact is that the

slender active hatchlings are quite arboreal. It is the adults of the water monitor that are preferentially aquatic. Such habitat partitioning of the varying sizes helps prevent cannibalism. Water monitors have been bred, but those in the pet trade of the world are collected from the wild. Up to two dozen eggs are laid, and the most successful incubation temperature seems to be between 83 and 86°F 28–30°C). Incubation duration is upwards of six months.

In keeping with their strongly arboreal tendencies, the babies of the water monitor are highly insectivorous. Tree-climbing crabs, snails, and other such invertebrates are also consumed. Baby water monitors also eat smaller lizards, snakes, and tree frogs, and would certainly not be averse to a meal of nestling birds or bird eggs, should the opportunity arise. If hungry, an adult water monitor will eat anything it can overpower or encounters. These lizards have been observed testing air currents, apparently on the trail of odoriferous carrion. Fish, mammals, turtles, hatchling crocodiles, and the eggs of birds and reptiles are also favored foods.

Unlike Nile monitors, which are noted for their foul dispositions, water monitors, if obtained young and worked with gently and diligently, can become very tame. One should always keep in mind, however, the terrible potential of the powerful jaws and claws. Until you are absolutely certain the lizard is not only tame, but tame with *you,* exercise caution.

Housing a monitor of such proportions may tax the ingenuity of a private keeper. Care of a lizard of this size by a private hobbyist will be greatly eased if the specimen is docile. In many cases, when it is available, a full room may be dedicated as a monitor enclosure. At the very least, an enclosure of 6 feet (2 m) in width and

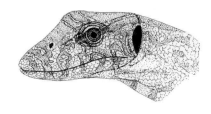

Nostrils of V. niloticus *vs. those of* V. salvator.

12 feet (4 m) (about half room size) in length will be necessary to house an adult. Basking areas warmed to 90–96°F (31–35.5°C), a hide-box, a very firmly affixed elevated shelf or tree trunk, and a large, easily cleaned water dish are the suggested cage furniture. While a single properly positioned heating bulb will suffice for juvenile water monitors, several heat bulbs will probably be necessary to allow an adult to thermoregulate effectively. Be certain that the bulbs are placed so your lizard cannot come in direct contact with them and sufficiently far from the water receptacle so they do not get splashed by the movement of the lizard.

Australian Monitors

Although Australia is the homeland of no fewer than 27 species of monitors (called "goannas" in Australia), comparatively few species are represented in private herpetoculture in other countries. Of the Australian monitors, a few species are fairly large, several are of moderate size, and many of them are small. Three species—the ridge-tailed (*V. acanthurus* ssp.), the Storr's (*V. storri* ssp.), and the Timor monitor (*V. timorensis* ssp.)—are well represented in private American collections. A few other species—rusty monitor (*V. kingorum*), Gould's monitor (*V. gouldii* ssp.) and the argus monitor (*V. panoptes* ssp.)—are also being bred by private hobbyists, but at present in very limited numbers. German hobbyists, seemingly far more advanced in the art of monitor breeding than their American counterparts, are producing at least small numbers of many additional species.

The Australian Ridge-Tailed Monitor, *V. acanthurus* ssp.

Once truly a rarity in the United States, the Australian ridge-tailed

V. salvator cumingi *is a Philippine race of Asian water monitor.*

It is the Asian water monitors from Thailand that most resemble the Nile monitor.

monitor, *V. acanthurus,* is now the species most frequently bred. Despite this, prices for this saxicolous desert species remain very high in America. It is also being bred in Europe, but remains expensive there too.

The ridge-tailed monitor is a beautiful spiny-tailed species that occasionally attains an adult size of 28 inches (71 cm). However, most seen in herpetoculture are well under that length.

V. kingorum.

71

The small Australian ridge-tailed monitor, V. a. acanthurus, *is now being captive-bred in some numbers.*

In fact, comparatively few specimens attain 20 inches (50 cm) in total length. Unlike many of the monitors more frequently seen by hobbyists, the ridge-tailed monitor does not have a long, slender, whiplike tail. The tail of *V. acanthurus* is rather short (approximately 1.5 times the snout-vent length), heavy, and prominently whorled with spiny, keeled scales. The ground color of the lizard is olive-brown. There are light longitudinal stripes on the nape and sides of the neck. Irregularly arranged light ocelli or spots on the trunk cause intricate reticulations of the dark pigment. Light rings alternate with dark on the tail. The rings are best defined on the basal three fifths of the tail length.

This species is found over much of the arid and semiarid northern half of Australia in deeply creviced escarpments and on stony plains. Besides the deep rock fissures they prefer, spiny-tailed monitors also seek protection beneath and between piled and jumbled boulders.

The Australian ridge-tailed monitor is represented by three rather poorly defined subspecies. The subspecies most commonly seen in the pet trade in America is also supposedly the most brightly colored. This is the nominate form, *V. a. acanthurus.* It occurs over much of northwestern Australia. The eastern race, *V. a. brachyurus,* is grayer and less brightly patterned. A very dark race, *V. a. insulanicus,* occurs only on Groot Eylandt (an island east of Arnhem Land, Northern Territory, in the Gulf of Carpentaria).

Although a desert/arid-land lizard, captive ridge-tailed monitors seem able to adapt to many differing conditions. They are not only being bred in fairly large numbers by private hobbyists in the semiarid southwestern United States, but have been bred in quasi-natural conditions in perpetually humid southwestern Florida as well.

Our breeding colonies in southwest Florida were maintained in 10-foot (3 m) diameter rings of aluminum. The aluminum was buried 12 inches (30 cm) into the ground and extended 24 inches (60 cm) above it. Into each enclosure was built a subterranean "maze" of retreats/hibernacula. Each enclosure held a huge jumble of native rough limestone boulders. We made at least two equally high basking stations (one for each male in each cage), that extended to the top of the aluminum or above it. Besides each pinnacle serving as the center of a territory for a male, the monitors that used these elevated stations were then able to keep a wary eye for approaching predators (of which they considered their keepers one). Despite their wariness, they were not as quick to disappear into the safety of their maze of boulders as some other monitor species.

This is another of the monitors that uses tripodal posturing to enable it to see a greater distance. By raising its head as high as possible above the surrounding obstructions, the monitors can spy approaching predators earlier.

We have not seen the males indulge in territorial displays while in the tripodal stance, but since many other monitor species do display this, ridge-tails probably do also.

We quickly learned that these monitors are sun worshippers. Although they might initially leave their refugia on warm overcast days, if startled they would again secrete themselves, seldom to venture forth again until the following day. On cool overcast days the monitors were seldom seen at all. In keeping with many other heliotherms, on hot sunny days the ridge-tailed monitors would bask in the morning and evening, retreating to their lairs during the very hottest hours. During these times, the basking rock surfaces might exceed 120°F (39°C). On cool days the *acanthurus* would bask throughout the day.

We found this species to be quite cold-tolerant. They required no additional winter heating while outside in southwest Florida. During the coldest weather these monitors would retire to their burrows and remain (often for days) until they sensed warmer weather had returned. However, if kept indoors, they should be kept warm. During the summer months, daytime highs of 88 to 94°F (31–34°C)—with a warmed basking spot of 106–110°F (41–43°C) are suggested. Nighttime temperatures may be allowed to drop into the low 70sF (21–23°C). Ambient winter temperatures may be a few degrees cooler, but the superheated daytime basking area should be retained.

Although territorial, if the caging is large enough and the cage furniture is properly arranged, more than a single male of this species may be kept with several females. This seems especially so when the lizards are kept indoors, where behavior is modified somewhat by the lack of natural sunlight. Even the best of the readily available full-spectrum bulbs produce little UV-A (the "natural behavior" ray) compared with Sol.

Egg size and egg quantity may vary with the size of the female monitor. Maximum clutch size is often quoted as 5, and the hatchlings are said to be "tiny" (total length of 2.5 inches (6.3 cm); Sprackland, 1992). However, we have had clutches from large females number up to 8 eggs and the hatchlings are somewhat more than 4 inches (10 cm) in total length. Admittedly, this is smaller than the small Storr's monitor, but it is larger than often reported.

Our eggs were incubated in slightly dampened sphagnum and hatched in from 81 to 90 days at "room temperature"—82–90°F (28–32°C). Hatchlings began eating suitably sized insects within 24 hours. A diet of commercially procured crickets, mealworms, waxworms, and butterworms was augmented with netsful of "field plankton" (insects that were netted locally in nearby insecticide-free, vacant grassy fields). Adults also ate pinky mice readily.

Storr's Monitor, *V. storri* ssp.

Although certainly not yet a commonly seen species, the attractive little spiny-tailed Storr's monitor, *V. storri,* has been bred in small numbers in the United States for more than 15 years. It is a rather common monitor in two disjunct areas of Australia. One population (*V. s. storri*) is present in northwestern Queensland and adjacent Northern Territory. The second population (*V. s. ocreatus*) occurs in northeastern Western Australia and adjacent Northern Territory. Between these two populations, one enters the range of a look-alike species, currently identified as *V. primordius*. However, the taxonomic status of *primordius* is uncertain. The two species differ only in the number of scales encircling the mid-body (*primordius* with 69 or fewer,

Although rather dark and obscurely marked, hobbyists eagerly seek the tiny Australian Storr's monitor, V. s. storri.

storri with 71 or more) and the fact that *primordius* is often a little darker. Hybrids between the two are known, muddying the taxonomic waters even more. *V. storri* is reddish-tan with a fine (but vague) pattern of darker reticulations. The spiny-tail of *V. storri* is unpatterned.

Storr's monitors are tiny—reportedly to 12 inches (30 cm)—but most are smaller. These are rock-dwelling monitors with a tail somewhat greater in length than the combined head and body length. They are hardy and easily kept.

Although we initially kept our colony of Storr's monitors indoors, we soon decided to build an outside pen for them. Like that for the ridge-tailed monitors, the pen was 10 feet (3 m) in diameter with aboveground walls 2 feet (.6 m) high. Below ground hibernacula were provided, as were three sizable piles of oolitic limestone boulders (one for each male). Besides utilizing the underground refugia, the monitors dug lengthy burrows of their own. Occasionally these would be started at the base of a boulder, but more often the lizards would dig hori-

zontally outward from an open side of the prepared underground refugia. These tunnels measured up to a yard (1 m) and were wide enough at the end to allow the lizard to reverse its position. The interactions between members of the group were interesting. The males were somewhat, but not persistently, territorial, usually satisfying themselves with posturing and threats rather than actual skirmishes. One male had set up territory on each of the three rock piles. The pinnacle rock of each of the piles was somewhat below the top of the two-foot (.6 m) high aluminum restraining wall of the enclosure. Because of this, the light of the rising sun would reach one of the piles a few minutes before it reached the other, while the rays of the setting sun would linger on another pile for a few minutes longer than on the other two. The monitors soon learned this. All would clamber from their nighttime refugia when the sun began to warm the aluminum wall of the enclosure. As the warming rays reached the first of the pinnacles, the females would all join the resident male to begin their daily regimen of basking. However, if the two males who had staked out the other piles attempted to approach, they were met by the resident male with threats and feints. These involved inflating or flattening his body, extending his legs, inflating the throat (gular) area and writhing the neck. The threats worked. No matter how much they wished to sun, the other males would scuttle away. But these two males soon learned another ploy that seemed to work as well for them. By assuming a tripodal stance—anterior almost fully erect—they could benefit from the sun at almost the same time the monitor across the cage did, and, since they were at home on their own rock piles, they experienced no aggressive interactions. In the evening, since the shadows would reach his rock pile first, by assuming the tripodal stance the male in shadow could take advantage of an additional few minutes of sunlight. In the several years that we had these interesting dwarf monitors, we never saw a female assume a tripodal position.

On overcast days, when temperatures were below 75°F (24°C), these monitors would seldom emerge from their refugia. Even on warmer, cloudy days their appearance above ground was often sporadic. On the other hand, if the sun was shining strongly, these monitors emerged from their refugia even on cold days, when air temperatures were in the 40s and 50sF (4–12°C). During such weather conditions they would bask virtually all day long. And on sunny days during our hot summers, when air temperatures would often near or reach 95°F (35°C)—the mid-afternoon surface temperature of the rock formations would hover at 120°F (49°C)—the Storr's monitors would bask in early morning and late afternoon, retiring to the coolness of their refugia when temperatures were the hottest.

Indoor summer daytime temperatures should vary from 88–94°F (31–34°C), with a brightly illuminated basking area of from 106 to 110°F (41–43°C). Nighttime temperatures can drop into the low 70sF (22°C). Winter temperatures a few degrees cooler may assist in reproductive cycling. The superwarmed daytime basking area should be retained. Photoperiods should also be lessened somewhat during the months of winter. A "natural" photoperiod seems best.

We successfully bred *V. s. storri* for the first time in 1981. This was, to our knowledge, the first time the species had been bred in captivity. They have since been captive-bred both in the United States and Europe.

One female, found inexplicably dead in her outside cage, contained 6 fully shelled, but still premature eggs. A few days later, on a morning following a very cold night, a pair of desiccated eggs were found near the mouth of a burrow. These were too desiccated and chilled to revitalize.

A single "good" egg was found at the cul-de-sac end of the foot-long (.3 m) burrow, beneath a torpid female *storri*. The egg was removed for incubation indoors. A closed margarine tub was used. The incubation medium was barely dampened sphagnum, but the humidity within the closed container was retained at 100 percent. At a temperature that fluctuated from 82 to 90°F (28–32°C), the egg hatched in 80 days.

Measuring 5³⁄₁₆ inches (13 cm) in overall length, the hatchling, which was precisely like the adults in coloration and pattern, was comparatively huge. The yolk sac had been fully utilized during incubation, and by the day following its hatching, the monitor was eagerly consuming crickets and other insects.

The growth of the hatchling was rapid, and the lizard was fully grown at about 8 months of age. Additional hatchlings in subsequent years confirmed most initial findings.

Although the adults of Storr's monitors were primarily insectivorous, eating crickets, caterpillars, grasshoppers, waxworms, and June beetles, they would readily consume the occasional pinky mice offered them. They also lapped eagerly at a honey-pureed fruit mixture that was periodically offered. Large shallow dishes of water were always available, but we never saw Storr's monitors do more than drink from them. After initially scattering as we approached, Storr's monitors would also drink droplets of water copiously from the rocks and plants when their enclosure was misted.

Timor monitors, V. t. timorensis, *are attractive but not awfully cold-tolerant.*

Because of its diminutive size and overall hardiness, we consider the Storr one of the finest of the occasionally available small monitor lizards. Unfortunately, its price remains prohibitively high and is apt to remain so until the lizards are captive-bred on a larger scale.

The Timor Monitor, *V. timorensis* ssp.

The Timor monitor, *V. timorensis,* is currently rather readily available in the pet trades of America and Europe at what is, for a small, coveted monitor, a moderate price. Two forms are currently being imported—one blackish with gold ocelli (some are dull and almost unicolored) and the other, although also variable, often blackish with a pattern of white to gray spots and ocelli (and seemingly a slightly different tail scalation). The former is the nominate form of the species and is classified as *V. t. timorensis.* This race occurs on the island of Timor, its satellite islands, and New Guinea. The latter form, long scientifically known as

V. t. similis, is now being considered a full species by many researchers. When this is done, the designation of "*timorensis*" is dropped from the name, and the lizard is referred to simply as *V. similis.* This pretty monitor occurs in northeastern Australia and, ostensibly, southern New Guinea, from which latter location it is being exported in some numbers. A third subspecies, *V. t. scalaris* (also considered a full species, *V. scalaris,* by some researchers), is found in northwestern Australia.

This, too, is a very pretty monitor, patterned with myriad small yellow spots on a dark, often nearly black ground. This form is not known to occur in captivity except in Australian collections.

Unless specified otherwise, the comments that follow apply specifically to our experience with *V. t. timorensis,* a monitor with which we worked for several years. However, they probably apply equally to both other subspecies.

The Timor monitor, a small, slender, arboreal monitor seldom attains 20 inches (50 cm) in total length. The long tail is at least 1.5 times the snout-vent length. It is a hardy species that has been bred in captivity on numerous occasions. The hatchlings are more brightly patterned than the adults; captives feed on a combination of insects, high quality canned cat food, pinky mice, and beaten eggs.

We have found Timor monitors to be less cold tolerant than certain other monitors from similar latitudes. In fact, Timors often continued placidly sunning on hot days, long after other species had retreated to their refugia. Although we did keep the Timors outdoors throughout the year in southwest Florida, we did learn that it was necessary to warm their underground refugia with a heat tape when temperatures plummeted. We used 55°F (13°C) as an arbitrary temperature below which the heat tapes were activated.

If maintained indoors, we suggest that the same temperature regimen as for other small monitors be used:

Daytime summer	86–94°F (30–34°C)
Nighttime summer	70–80°F (21–27°C)
Daytime winter	78–86°F (25.5–30°C)
Nighttime winter	68–74°F (20–23°C)

A basking area warmed to 104–110°F (40–43°C) should be available daytimes throughout the year. A "normal" photoperiod (less in winter, more in summer) should be provided.

In the wild, these are highly arboreal monitors, which forage, rest, and probably breed in the trees. They are active and quick. These characteristics are carried over into captivity. Timor monitors are excellent jumpers,

and are more adept at escaping their enclosures than many other monitor species. If these monitors are kept indoors, a large, vertically oriented cage should be provided.

We have found Timor monitors housed in "naturalistic" outdoor settings to be much more alert and unapproachable than many other monitor species. We have also found that, since trees would be difficult for us to provide, Timor monitors adapt very well to life in rock piles. Those that we maintained never tamed, being as ready to flee at our approach after several years in captivity as they were on the day they were received. We also found that these lizards had voracious appetites, and none was reluctant to eat half-grown or even larger mice, lizards such as anoles and skinks that would wander into their cage, as well as large and seemingly unpalatable beetles and bugs. They also readily consumed vitamin-and-mineral-enhanced canned cat foods of many flavors. A fairly large flat bowl of water was always available, and occasionally the Timor monitors would enter and soak for short periods. However, even when soaking, these lizards were always ready to dart for cover at the slightest disturbance.

After watching the interactions of male Timor monitors caged communally indoors, we thought them quite tolerant of each other. After moving the lizards to outside facilities, we were quickly disabused of this notion. Once in the natural unfiltered sunlight, the males became so agonistic towards each other that we could keep only one per 10-foot (3 m) diameter cage. The females remained amiable, however.

When displaying or apparently just trying to see for a longer distance, the males would assume a tripodal stance, standing upright on their rear legs while supported by their tail. If in a territorial dispute, while the lizards were erect, their body would be either flattened and tilted towards the interloper or inflated, their head would be angled downward, the throat inflated, the tongue extended for several seconds at a time, and the neck and anterior body moved in sinuous undulations. Males would occasionally grapple while in this upright position. Aggression was also evident while the lizards were in their more normal four-footed posture. Then the body was inflated somewhat and flattened vertically, the body and neck would be "humped," the gular area inflated, and the head would be held at a curious angle. The tongue was often extended for several seconds. The territorial dispute was usually settled without actual combat.

During the time that we had Timor monitors, we found two nests of eggs. One consisted of 6, and the other of 4 eggs. The hatchlings were very slender, somewhat more brightly colored, voracious, 5-inch (13 cm) diminutive replicas of the adults.

Currently, besides those mentioned earlier, a few monitor species once considered rare, or, at least unobtainable by private owners, are also available to hobbyists. Because of their dwindling numbers in nature, wild monitors will probably not be available in the pet trade for many more years. In the interim it is up to us to ferret out the secrets of their private lives. Only in this way will we ascertain that any remain available for future hobbyists to enjoy.

The Komodo Dragon

The World's Largest Lizard

Although this magnificent lizard is certainly *not* a pet species, there is so much mysticism and so many inaccuracies attributed to this species that no discussion of monitors is complete without at least a cursory mention. Most up-to-date knowledge of the species has been provided us by Dr. Walter Auffenberg of the Florida Museum of Natural History.

The heavy-set and terrestrial Komodo dragon, *V. komodoensis,* is unquestionably the world's bulkiest lizard. Record size is 10 feet 2.5 inches (3.2 m).

Komodo dragons are restricted in distribution to a few islands in the East Indies. Besides the already mentioned great length (attained by males), weights in excess of 440 pounds (200 kg) have been recorded.

Komodo dragons have long been considered an endangered species. Exportation of specimens from their homeland in the Flores Islands is carefully restricted. Only occasionally have accredited zoos or museums been able to acquire specimens, and until very recently, since none had been bred in captivity, those specimens acquired were considered "dead-end" creatures. But now the National Zoo (Washington, DC) has successfully bred Komodo dragons, and a joint breeding program between the National Zoo and the Cincinnati Zoo in Ohio has begun, and produced offspring.

In color, the adult dragons are nearly a uniform reddish-brown, darkest on the head and forelimbs. In contrast, the hatchlings are brightly banded with dark chevrons from the rear of their head to their shoulders, light-on-dark ocellations on the rear limbs, banded forelimbs, and a banded tail. The young are quite arboreal, a feature that separates them in the wild from the possibility of cannibalism by the terrestrial adults.

Captive adults seem to recognize their keepers and certainly adapt well to existing conditions. It was the conditions that had to be adapted to them to induce the successful breeding programs. Watching the adult dragons attack and devour proffered goat carcasses has become a tourist attraction on certain of the islands to which the species is native. Despite this "hokey," there is no question that Komodo dragons are top-of-the-line predators that are more than capable of securing themselves—from all but humans.

It is only recently that the Komodo dragon, V. komodoensis, *has been bred in captivity. Compare this juvenile with the adult pictured on page 50.*

The Earless Monitor

Family Lanthanotidae

Genus *Lanthanotus;* Bornean Earless Monitor

There remain few lizards as poorly understood as the Bornean earless monitor, *Lanthanotus borneensis,* the sole resident of this family and genus. Captive and preserved specimens have yielded physical data on size and scalation, but nearly everything else in print, including what is written here, is speculation.

The facts: Specimens have been collected only in the Sarawak and western Kalimantan regions of northern Borneo. Those specimens measure up to slightly more than 15 inches (38 cm) in total length. Since most specimens have been smaller, it is thought that the 15-inchers were large adults. The earless monitor is the color of wet earth. The head scales are small and rather flat. The head is slightly depressed temporally and barely wider than the neck. The body scales are beadlike with several longitudinal rows of strongly tuberculate scales. Of these, a dorsolateral row on each side are the most prominently tuberculate. While less greatly enlarged, the vertebral scales are prominent.

When hurried, *Lanthanotus* folds its proportionately small legs against its sides and relies primarily on side to side undulations, a form of transport that would serve equally well in terrestrial, aquatic, and loose soil conditions. When unhurried in terrestrial situations the fully functional legs are used in traditional manner, dragging the daschund-shaped body along.

It is also known that lanthanotids are not at all hesitant to enter water, are capable of remaining submerged for lengthy periods, drink copiously, and desiccate rapidly if denied water. They can swim strongly. The eyes are reduced in size, but have fully functional lids. The lower lid has a transparent window allowing a degree of vision while closed. Thus the eye is largely protected. The nostrils are dorsally situated; an external ear opening is lacking. The tail lacks fracture planes and is probably not, or only poorly, regenerated if lost through accident. The tail of *Lanthanotus* is semiprehensile. The tongue is protrusible and rather deeply bifurcated. The teeth are recurved and sharply pointed. The lizard is oviparous.

The natural history reported for the Bornean earless lizard is speculation. It is thought that they are creatures of moist habitats, perhaps even largely aquatic. It is thought that rather than rare (as has so often been reported) they are merely secretive, remaining burrowed deeply in loose, organic soils and decomposing vegetable matter. It is thought that they frequent the warm shallows of flooded rice paddies

L. borneensis.

and the drainage ditches near the paddies. It is known that most collected specimens have come from such areas, but this may be due to faulty collection data or lack of sampling in other areas.

Captives have not fared particularly well. Perhaps this is due to stress during shipping. Captives have fed on both bird and reptile eggs as well as worms and some fish.

The Bornean earless lizard is rare in captivity. Over the last few years, the Cincinnati Zoo in Ohio has acquired several specimens. They are, of course, striving to learn about the lizards, but they too, are finding *Lanthanotus* to be delicate and difficult captives. However, because of the efforts of the zoo, perhaps soon we will be able to move some of our thoughts from the "speculations" to the "known-with-certainty" column.

A Brief Checklist of Eagerly Sought, but Hard-to-Acquire Monitors

The pygmy mulga monitor, *V. gilleni,* is a slender arboreal and saxicolous species of the arid interior of the Australian continent. It is gray anteriorly, on the lower sides, and on the tail and reddish dorsally. The dark dorsal and basal tail marking are coalesced into vaguely delineated crossbars, and the distal tail markings are rather well-defined longitudinal stripes. Once rarely seen outside of its native

This argus monitor is standing erect to enable it to see above the grasses.

country, the pygmy mulga monitor has now been bred by both American and European hobbyists and zoos. It is occasionally available from specialist dealers.

Of the Australian monitors, the large Gould's monitor, *V. gouldii* is best known to the general populace of the world. Also referred to as the "sand monitor" (or "goanna"), this is the species most often seen on TV screens grappling in territorial disputes, careening off in bipedal bursts of speed, or standing partially or virtually erect in a tripodal defensive or scanning position. When the stance is assumed for defensive purposes, the gular area is prominently distended and the tongue lolls. When standing merely to observe its surroundings, the throat is not distended and the tongue is actively protruded and withdrawn. *V. gouldii* is found in suitably arid or subarid habitats over all except the extreme southeast of the Australian continent. It attains a total length of about 5 feet (1.5 m). The tail, which is about one and a half times the snout-vent length, is heavy, and used with lashlike efficiency against approaching adversaries. Rounded basally, the distal half of the tail is laterally compressed and has paired dorsal keels. In keeping with their largely terrestrial habits, Gould's monitors are a heavy-bodied species, even more so after a sizable meal.

These monitors seem most at home in or near considerable ground cover, and even the most brightly colored among them virtually disappear when sitting quietly amidst the dappled shade of a desert thicket. They are of variable ground color, but they are usually similar in color to the desert sands over which they race.

The specimens from Australia's arid, red sand desert interior are known subspecifically as *V. g. flavirufus.* They tend to have bright reds, russets, and yellows incorporated into their dorsal colors. Since most hobbyists feel that this is the prettier subspecies, and since it is the more uncommon in collections, it is particularly coveted. *V. g. gouldii* is more variable. It may be an almost unicolored tan or olive-brown or strikingly patterned in transverse rows of large cream spots against a nearly black ground color. Both subspecies have an often prominent dark temporal stripe, and both tend to have a light unmarked tailtip. The young of both subspecies tend to be the brightest, while older *V. g. gouldii* tend toward the dullest coloration and least pattern.

Although it is well represented in both private collections and zoos of the world, the Gould's monitor is still too uncommonly seen to be considered a "pet store favorite."

It has now been bred on several occasions, both by American and European herpetoculturists. Despite its large size, Gould's monitor seems to produce a comparatively small clutch of rather large eggs. The numbers most frequently mentioned vary between four and eight. This small maximum number may be due as much to a lack of research as to actuality.

To get some idea of the appearance of *V. kingorum,* envision a Storr's monitor with a proportionately long,

The desert Gould's monitor, V. gouldii flavirufus, *is more brilliantly colored than the nominate form.*

Despite its pallid coloration, the pygmy mulga monitor, V. gilleni, *is a favorite of hobbyists.*

nonspinose tail. Although *V. kingorum* is now being bred by a handful of private American and European hobbyists, it will remain a comparative rarity for many years. It is known to occur only among fissured sandstone outcroppings and escarpments in the Kimberley region, basically at the junction of Western Australia and Northern Territory. *V. kingorum* is a wary, seldom seen monitor that is quick to retreat deeply into the safety of the fissures of its rock homeland when frightened. The long tail accounts for nearly two thirds of this species 15-inch (38 cm) total length. The caudal scales are heavily keeled, but not spinose. The reddish dorsum is patterned with vaguely delineated irregular darker markings in the form of ocelli, rosettes, or simple spots, several scales in size. On the distal two-thirds of the tail the spots may form vague broken stripes.

The 4-four (1.2 m) length of the males of Merten's water monitor, *V. mertensi,* makes them dramatically larger than their mates. This is one of the very few monitor species in which sexual dimorphism is pronounced. Besides size differences, a difference in "face" coloration often occurs. Sexually mature males develop a blue suffusion to the sides of the face, while the females develop a pale orange. The overall ground color is olive-gray to olive-brown or black. Tiny yellow spots are present on the posterior nape, the trunk, limbs, and tail. This is a highly aquatic species that spends a great deal of time in the water and most of the remaining time very near it. In keeping with this, it feeds on crustaceans, mollusks, and fish as well as the "usual" monitor fare.

Although small numbers of this species are regularly bred, incubation or other problems have resulted in poor hatches and malformed young. Research continues. This species occurs along watercourses in the northern quarter of Australia.

Because of its intricate pattern of eye-like spots, *V. panoptes* is often referred to as the argus monitor. There are three currently recognized subspecies, *panoptes* and *rubidus* of Australia and *horni* of New Guinea. This is one of the most beautiful and intricately patterned of the larger Australian/New Guinean monitors. Until 1980, this species was thought to be merely one of the many color phases of the widespread and variable Gould's monitor. The argus monitor tops out at about 4 feet (1.2 m) in length, a slightly smaller adult size than that attained by the very similar Gould's monitor. The tail of the argus monitor, which is rounded basally and strongly compressed, is about 1.5 times the SVL. The tail bears two prominent dorsal keels.

If threatened and escape seems difficult, the argus monitor inflates its throat and lolls the tongue out. It may utilize this defensive display while either in the normal four-footed stance or, after assuming a tripodal position, propped erect on rear legs and tail. While still on all fours, the argus monitor will also lash an adversary strongly with its tail. If escape becomes possible, the lizard will dash off, first on all fours, then, when "up to speed," bipedally.

In Australia, the pretty yellow-spangled *panoptes* has a much smaller range than does *V. gouldii.* As far as is currently known, the ranges of the two subspecies are widely separated. However, the presence in collections of a very few specimens from intermediate areas between the main ranges suggests that additional observation would benefit our knowledge.

V. p. panoptes occurs over the northern fifth of Australia. It is the darker form and is often patterned with bands of discrete yellow spots arranged in regular to irregular fashion. Prominent-to-obscure bands of smaller black spots often alternate between the yellow. Other specimens are liberally peppered with light scales among the dark and have well-defined light ocelli haphazardly scattered over both dorsal and lateral surfaces. The tail is banded to the tip.

V. p. rubidus is the race encountered in coastal and inland central Western Australia. Although the pattern is quite similar to that of the nominate race, the dorsal and lateral surfaces of this subspecies are usually washed with sand-red and the terminal one fifth of the tail is straw yellow to cream and unbanded.

Range alone will identify the southern New Guinean *V. p. horni*. This is fortunate, for this race is very like the Australian *V. p. panoptes* in overall appearance. The majority of the specimens seen in the pet trade of the United States are shipped from New Guinea.

V. panoptes is an active monitor. Although primarily terrestrial, it can climb if necessary and is perfectly able to swim. It seems more predisposed to mesic (an area with moderate moisture) and riparian habitats than the Gould's monitor. This species has now been bred by European hobbyists.

Introduction to the Teiids

The family Teiidae includes the tegus, caiman lizards, race runners, whiptails, and several lesser-known genera. All are exclusively of New World distribution. (Many genera once in Teiidae are now placed by some taxonomists in the rather recently proposed family, the Gymnophthalmidae.)

Teiids are much more abundant in the West Indies and Latin America than in North America. Only the six-lined race runner and the whiptails of the genus *Cnemidophorus* are found in the United States.

Look-alikes: In the new restricted sense, the family Teiidae now contains only nine genera of lizards that are of similar appearance but vastly dissimilar size. They are those once called "macroteiids" by taxonomists. The more common genera are *Tupinambis*,

Most tegus are of rather similar appearance and habits. The Amazonian black and yellow tegu, Tupinambis teguixin, *is the species most often seen in the pet trade.*

the tegus; *Dracaena*, the persistently aquatic caiman lizards; *Callopistes*, the dwarf and monitor tegus; *Cnemidophorus*, the whiptails and race runners; *Kentropyx*, the forest whiptails; and *Ameiva*, also referred to as whiptails or "jungle runners."

The big three: Of those nine genera, only four are seen with any regularity in the pet trade. Of these, we will discuss only "the big three"—the tegus, caiman lizards, and the dwarf tegu. The fourth genus, the ameivas, contains a large number of species, but has not yet become popular in herpetoculture.

The members of Teiidae are found in the New World, from the southern United States southward through South America and the West Indies. They range in size from just 1½ to 18 inches (3.7–45 cm). Body form may be stout to slender, but not as attenuated as the monitors. Stout species tend to have a large head and well-developed limbs (the caiman lizards), while the more slender types have a small head with reduced limbs (the tegus and dwarf tegu). Usually the snout is pointed and the tail fragile. Ears may be open (whiptails, ameivas, and race runners) or covered with scales (tegus, caiman lizards, and dwarf tegu). The various whiptails or race runners are often considered analagous, both in appearance and ecology, with the Old World lacertid lizards.

The larger, truly macroteiids are usually compared in appearance and behavior with the monitors. Like the

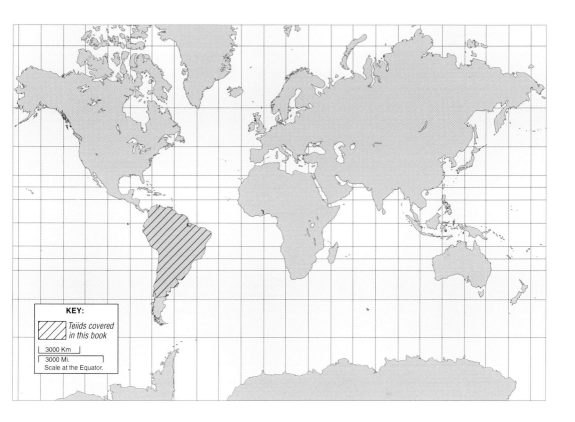

KEY:

Teiids covered
in this book

3000 Km

3000 Mi.
Scale at the Equator.

monitors, many of these lizards may rise onto their hind legs to see above obstructions. When in this position, their tail is used as a support. Besides this tripodal stance, teiids are fully capable of running bipedally when startled. In addition to being collected alive for the pet industry, the larger teiids are killed for their skins that are featured in lizard-skin boots and shoes, hatbands, and wallets.

Diet and behavior: All teiids are generally very adept at finding insects and other prey. Fruits and palm nuts are also readily eaten. These lizards fully utilize not only visual, but tactile and chemo-sensory prey location techniques. It is likely that auditory cues play a part in prey location, for

Teiid in tripodal pose.

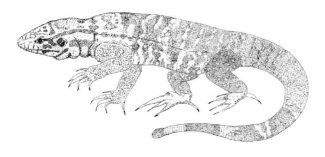

Teiid with front foot raised as a sign of territoriality.

teiids are able to locate, then unearth burrowing beetle larvae that seem to be making no visible signs on the surface. A rapid scratching with the front feet is used to uncover subterranean prey once it is located. A similar motion, but this time with just a single foot waved above the surface of the ground, is used to indicate nervousness (as immediately prior to a dash to safety) and as a territorial signal to an approaching interloping male.

Despite being thought of as terrestrial lizards, many species, including the tegus and caiman lizards, have been observed foraging in trees, and the nests of some have been found excavated into arboreal termitaria. The caiman lizards are semiaquatic.

Teiids are as adept at noting and defining potential danger as they are at foraging. Their dashes to safety are often along established trails. All are accomplished burrowers, usually constructing lengthy home burrows to which they regularly return.

Three Teiid Genera

The Dwarf Tegu and Monitor Tegu, *Callopistes*

This genus of macroteiids—*Callopistes*—contains two species of dissimilar appearance. Both are intermediate in appearance between a large whiptail and a small tegu, and can be distinguished from the tegus by the absence of femoral pores. These are alert lizards that, once treated for their normally heavy load of endoparasites, can be hardy and long-lived. The pet trade often refers to the less colorful of the two species, *C. flavipunctatus,* as the monitor tegu, in reference to its monitorlike appearance. The very attractive *C. maculatus* is known as the dwarf tegu. The old males of both species develop heavy jowls.

Both species are terrestrial and inhabit rocky, sparsely vegetated, arid to semiarid steppes on the Pacific slopes of the Andes chain. They are oviparous. They eagerly accept insects. *C. flavipunctatus* also preys heavily on smaller lizards. Both tropical and palm fruits are also eaten. Acclimated captives of both species may accept small mice and canned cat food or reptile foods. Although not as "flighty" as whiptails, these lizards may injure their snouts by darting headlong into the sides of their terraria. Until they become used to your presence, it may be necessary to cover the glass terrarium sides with paper. This will not only offer the lizards security, but will allow them to become familiar with the otherwise not always easily discerned glass barriers.

C. flavipunctatus

The monitor tegu, the larger of the two species, occasionally attains 40 inches (100 cm) in total length. Tail length is about 200 percent of the SVL. This lizard might best be described as of drab coloration. The ground color is of a variable gray patterned with equally variable darker reticulations and mottlings. The crown of the head is darker than the nape and body. This is not a particularly pretty lizard—a fact often reflected by the extended time that most spend at the dealerships that import them. However, they do tame quickly and are then easily handled.

Range: This is an Ecuadorian and Peruvian species.

C. maculatus

In contrast to its larger relative, the dwarf tegu is a pretty species that sells readily when it is available. It is a Chilean species that reaches 19 inches (48 cm). The dorsum is russet and bears four longitudinal rows of light-edged dark ocelli. The scales of the tail are large and like those of all teiids, arranged in prominent rings. The tail is duller than the dorsum and dark-spotted. The sides are lighter than the dorsum, the venter is light, and both sides and venter are flecked with darker pigment.

Habitats and habits: Well-adapted to extremes of weather and temperature, these lizards occur from the open, sun-baked, rocky littoral areas to elevations of about 1,500 feet (500 m) in the foothills of the Andes. They reportedly bask extensively in the

Although now only sporadically available, the dwarf tegu, Callopistes maculatus, *is hardy and long-lived in captivity.*

intense sunlight. Certainly captives enjoy basking, flattening themselves beneath their heat lamps, with limbs extended and eyes closed. They appreciate a well-illuminated daytime basking area that approaches a surface temperature of 100°F (38°C) and as long as the lizards can readily retreat from the area of intense heat when necessary, the surface temperature of the basking spot can even be allowed to near 105°F (40.5°C). The remainder of the terrarium should be in the 85–90°F (29–32°C) range. Nighttime temperatures can be allowed to drop rather radically.

When frightened, these lizards run bipedally. Although an occasional

The caiman lizard, Dracaena guianensis, *is a large, highly aquatic, very specialized teiid of the Amazon drainage.*

female, imported gravid, has laid eggs, seemingly few have been successfully incubated. Successful captive breedings are even rarer. It is likely that a lengthy period of full winter dormancy is necessary to induce breeding by either of these teiid lizards. Since neither species is imported frequently any longer, it would behoove herpetoculturists to quickly learn the basics necessary to realize breeding success with the two *Callopistes.*

The Caiman Lizards, *Dracaena* sp.

This is a bitypic genus of big—to 40 inches (1 m)—semiaquatic lizards with oversized heads and powerful jaws. The teeth are blunted and the posterior molarlike teeth have flattened surfaces suitable for crushing the shells of the large snails on which these lizards feed.

Appearance: The ventral scales are heavy and platelike. Above them on the sides are smaller, tubercle-studded lateral scales. The dorsal surface is clad in large, tubercular scales that are encircled by varying numbers of smaller ones. The brownish *D. paraguayensis* has a more extensive dorsal studding than the greener *D. guianensis.* The heads of both tend to be orange and the tails of both are laterally flattened but not so extensively as that of the related *Crocodilurus lacertinus.* The tails of the caiman lizards are heavy, keeled, and pointed.

Habitats and habits: Powerful swimmers, caiman lizards spend much of their time in the water and the rest of their time basking in the sunlight near the water or actually atop rafts of vegetation. The basking undoubtedly helps deter many of the fungal and bacterial skin infections often associated with aquatic reptiles.

These are oviparous lizards; according to report, they typically utilize termite nests in which to deposit their eggs.

Diet: The two species, *D. guianensis* and *D. paraguayensis* are usually referred to as specialist feeders on gastropod mollusks. In the wild, however, individuals have been seen eating both insects and fish, so perhaps they are more opportunistic feeders than is generally thought. Captives have been known to eat some prepared foods. Among other things, canned fish-flavored cat foods, smelts and other fish, and large insects are accepted. Despite this, both species are considered somewhat difficult to keep and care for.

D. guianensis was once imported in fair numbers for the pet trade. After a lengthy hiatus, it is again being seen in small numbers in reptile shipments from Suriname. We hope, we will learn enough about their needs to keep at least some successfully. The durable skins of these lizards continue to be used in the leather industry.

Tegus, *Tupinambis* sp.

Before getting into a discussion of the tegus, let's review current tegu nomenclature. Although unimportant to a pet shop customer who sees the animal, likes the way it looks, and then buys it, the scientific names are important to a hobbyist making a phone purchase. Hobbyists may be unfamiliar with most of the scientific names used in this book. However, the names used here are the most valid at the time of writing, and their usage will probably be generally adopted over the next few years.

These scientific names are very different from those long in use and seemingly well entrenched, and from the relatively recent nomenclatural changes made in 1973 by W. Presch in a paper entitled "A Review of the Tegus, Lizard Genus *Tupinambis* (Sauria: Teiidae) from South America." His paper synonymized names and reduced species of tegus from four to two.

A more recent study by T.C.S. Avila-Pires has described one new species, resurrected another, and altered some scientific names. It is her proposal that we have used here. The Amazonian tegu has been split from the more southerly one (but under new or reassigned names) and a new species has been described. Her statement that there are yet undescribed species within this genus may well be prophetic.

As documented by Avila-Pires, the tegus, *Tupinambis,* now contain the following species (the parenthetical names are those by which they were formerly known):

Amazonian tegu, *T. teguixin* (*nigropunctatus*)

Southern tegu, *T. merianae* (*teguixin*).

Red tegu, *T. rufescens*

Black-banded tegu, *T. longilineus* (a newly described species, not found in herpetoculture)

T. duseni, a very poorly known species from, and perhaps endemic to, Parana, Brazil

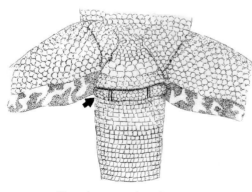

Cloacal spurs-male red tegu.

With that said, let's move on to a discussion of the lizards themselves.

Of all of the teiids, the tegus are most sought by both casual hobbyists and herpetoculturists. The tegus are well known and readily recognized. In gross external appearance the tegus resemble a heavy-bodied, big-headed monitor lizard. The two greatest differences are in the type of body scalation and in the arrangement and configuration of the tail scalation. The scales in which a tegu is clad dorsally and laterally are relatively small, flattened, and rather shiny, and become larger on the underneath or venter. The tail is unkeeled, with scales that are arranged in prominent whorls.

The adult black and yellow, white, or reddish tegus can be mistaken for few other lizards. The genus that most closely approaches them in appearance are the confamilial caiman lizards, *Dracaena*. However, the caiman lizards have lines of large tuberculate scales mixed in with the smaller dorsal and lateral scales and have a keeled, compressed tail as well. *Dracaena* is largely aquatic; *Tupinambis* is preferentially terrestrial, but is well able to climb.

The members of *Tupinambis* have both femoral and preanal pores. Males may be identified by the presence of a small postanal spur on each side of the tail base. These are usually composed of three barely protruding ventrolateral scales. Although small, the spurs are easily visible if the lizard is in hand.

Of the tegus, the black and white and the red that are the most cold-tolerant. Since it is these two that occur the farthest south—the most temperate regions in the range of the genus—this tolerance is understandable.

Breeding: Although tegus are bred in captivity, captive reproduction is not yet considered routine. Additionally, the majority of successes have been had by breeders who routinely maintain their lizard colonies outdoors. A certain amount of extrapolation is needed for breeding the lizards indoors.

It would seem that a period of cooling (and quite probably, hibernation) is very important when cycling the red and the black and white tegus reproductively. A natural photoperiod is probably only slightly less important. It is probable, but not certain, that seasonal temperature and photoperiod changes so important to the red and the black and white tegus are less important to cycling the more equatorial black and yellow tegu. At and near the equator, neither temperature nor photoperiod alter significantly throughout the year. Rather, the reproductive cycling for the Amazonas forms may well be stimulated more by humidity and rainfall variations that would most effectively simulate the rainy and dry seasons of the equatorial regions. However, the ambient temperature should be lowered slightly during the drier periods, but the warmed basking area should be provided daily. Night temperatures should be a few degrees lower than those maintained during the day. This is often accomplished automatically when the basking lamp is turned off for the night.

Because imported specimens have remained readily available and inexpensive, black and yellow tegus, *T. teguixin*, have served as the introductory species of this lizard genus for many hobbyists. Ready availability, however, seldom means that a lizard is well adapted to captivity. This is certainly the case with most imported black and yellow tegus—especially those large specimens that have been captured and imported. These large—commonly to 3 feet (1 m)—and powerful lizards usually remain "flighty," will scratch with their claws and whip with their tails if handled, and will bite

Both the babies and adults of the Amazonian black and yellow tegu are imported for the pet trade. This species can be difficult to tame.

savagely and void excrement on their handler if carelessly restrained. This is not exactly an ideal set of characteristics for a budding hobbyist to encounter. However, if obtained while young and handled frequently and carefully, black and yellow tegus can become quite tractable.

Because imported black and yellow tegus do remain inexpensive, no extensive efforts have yet been made by herpetoculturists to breed them.

Red tegus, T. rufescens, *are uncommon in the pet trade, but eagerly sought by collectors. Males of this massive Argentine lizard species are larger and more brightly colored than the females.*

Most of the specimens available have either been captured from the wild or are hatched from eggs laid by freshly collected gravid females. An incubation temperature of from 83–86°F (28–30°C) will result in hatchlings emerging in from approximately 120 to more than 170 days, a much longer incubation duration than is known for other more temperate tegu species. This lengthy incubation period is difficult to explain, for of all of the tegus, the climatic conditions at the latitude where the black and yellow tegu occurs seem the most equable for rapid incubation. Perhaps embryonic development temporarily ceases during the dry season. Such a diapause is well documented in other reptiles.

In the United States, the two most commonly bred tegu species are the red and the black and white.

The two most successful breeders of these tegus are Glades Herp, Inc. of Ft. Myers, Florida (red tegus), and

Agama International, Inc. of Montevallo, Alabama (black and white tegus). Both of these breeders maintain their breeding specimens outdoors year round. Should you decide to set up an outside facility, remember that tegus are powerful lizards; they are efficient diggers, can climb reasonably well, and will constantly investigate the walls of their cage for weakened areas. These lizards can and will swim.

During the winter months, protected facilities are provided for the lizards. Glades Herp, Inc. provides a heated hide-box but not a substrate sufficiently deep for their red tegus to dig hibernating burrows. Agama provides no heated hide-box, but provides up to 2 feet (.6 m) of soil into which the black and white tegus burrow deeply, and usually communally, to hibernate.

In both cases, the lizards' appetites begin to drop off in the early autumn and the lizards cease feeding shortly thereafter. Since cold weather comes to Alabama earlier and lasts longer than it does in southern Florida, the black and white tegus at Agama International hibernate for the longer time. Owners Bert and Hester Langerwerf estimate that their black and white tegus eat about four and a half months of the twelve, are active for about another month and a half, and are in actual hibernation for at least six months of the year. Perhaps it is the waning photoperiod that dictates the activity cycle of the Langerwerfs' tegus, for the animals prepare and retire to their hibernacula while daytime temperatures are still in the upper 80sF (31°C).

At Glades Herp, Chuck Hurt, who cares for the breeding farm, has noted that their red tegus are inactive for about three and a half months out of each year. Like the black and whites, the red tegus cease feeding a few weeks before actually beginning their hibernation.

The lizards breed shortly after emerging from hibernation. Female tegus are quite unlike most other lizards, because they actually construct a nest of leaves, straw, and other ground debris to accommodate their eggs. In captivity, the observed females nudged and dragged the provided nesting material under their enclosure shelters, constructing bulky nests prior to egg deposition.

Glades Herp provides a covered, earth-filled nesting box for their red tegus. This system proved entirely acceptable to the big lizards, which have been bred for two recent consecutive years. The clutches of eggs (all numbering in the low to mid-20s), have hatched in from 77 to 92 days at an average incubation temperature of 84°F (29°C). The hatchlings measured nearly 10 inches (25 cm) in total length and, while not brightly colored, were attractive. With brownish-red and black crossbands, the hatchlings were of very different color from the hatchlings of either the black and yellow or the black and white tegus.

Red tegu adults, *T. rufescens,* are variably colored. In general, they are black lizards with profuse-to-sparse light markings. The light areas may be just on the reddish side of white or actually quite a bright red. Adult males are usually a much brighter red than the females and may actually have even much of the black suffused with red. The color of the light bands of the females may vary from a muddy-brown to cream-brown, but is seldom truly red.

The red tegu is of western Argentine distribution. Besides being large—30 to about 40 inches (75–100 cm)—the red tegu is of robust build. Despite their large size, red tegus are relatively gentle lizards and are quick to accept humans as nonthreatening. Some specimens can actually be called tame.

Hurt has noted that the disposition of the relatively placid gravid females became increasingly agonistic as the laying date neared.

The black and white tegu, *T. merianae,* is arguably the longest of the tegus. Specimens of 4 feet (1.2 m) in length have been reported. Like the red tegu, with advancing age the black and white tegu attains a great bulk.

The Langerwerfs noted the same increase in agonistic behavior with their gravid female black and white tegus. As the laying date approached, the tegus become formidably aggressive.

The conditions provided at Agama International for the breeding of their black and white tegus are somewhat more "natural" than most captive conditions. The Langerwerfs provided loose straw, and found the female utilized the straw in the nest construction. The female black and white tegu dug deeply, lining the nesting chamber with straw. She then laid and covered the eggs and made an "attendance" chamber above the eggs. The female was tightly coiled in the top chamber when found by the Langerwerfs. She was protecting her clutch of 52 eggs!

At 80 to 85°F (27–29°C) incubation lasted for about 65 days. The hatchlings of the black and white tegu are suffused dorsally and laterally with bright green. This distinctive color fades rapidly and may be gone entirely after the second shedding.

T. merianae ranges widely over temperate southern and subtropical South America. It is known from Argentina, Brazil, and Uruguay.

Despite their great size, even the adults of tegus are alert, easily startled lizards. We have met the black and yellow tegu in forest clearings and along forest edges in Venezuela, Colombia, and Peru, and marveled at how unapproachable the big lizards were. While we were still binocular-distance away, the basking adults would come to attention. A few more steps on our part and the anterior of the body would be lifted. Once that happened it took only a gentle movement from us—in any direction—to send the lizards cascading headlong into the surrounding forest. We could hear their retreat long after the lizards had disappeared from sight. The closest we ever got to one in the wild was when we surprised a black and yellow tegu on the far side of a log over which we were stepping. The big lizard reacted with gaping jaws and slashing tail. The lizard fled a short distance and disappeared into a burrow (probably of its own making) at the base of a shrub.

Most tegus make hardy pets. Many, especially the Amazonians, imported at adult size, fail to tame, however. These will bite, scratch, and whip with their powerful tail if you attempt to handle them. Any one of these defenses can be painful to a potential handler.

Glades Herp, Inc. of Ft. Myers, Florida has succeeded in breeding red tegus. Their specimens are maintained outdoors year round.

Because of their great adult size, tegus require large caging facilities. Many persons allow a tame tegu the run of a room. In the hotter southerly climes, tegus are often kept in screen rooms or pool areas. If the screen goes all the way to the ground you will have to reinforce it to assure that your lizard will be restrained. Indoors, many are kept in cages that incorporate a full sheet of plywood as the bottom.

Although not particularly agile climbers, tegus have been reported

The southern black and white tegu has been recently redescribed as T. merianae. Agama International of Montevallo, Alabama has bred this species.

in arboreal situations. This fact, plus the ability of tegus to jump upwards, must be considered when their caging is being designed. Although a simple interior overhang will prevent their escape from a cage with suitably tall sides, a full cage cover remains the best way to assure containment of your tegus.

Daytime cage temperatures should be in the 77 to 85°F (25–29°C) range, with an illuminated basking area of 95 to 103°F (35–40°C) on one end. Night temperatures may be allowed to drop somewhat. The two southernmost tegus are best able to withstand truly cold temperatures. The big black and white tegus have overwintered in outdoor enclosures as far north in the United States as Birmingham, Alabama.

Tegus are opportunistic feeders both in nature and in captivity. Rodents, insects, nestling birds, some prepared foods, and some vegetation are accepted. Tegus seem to prefer succulent fruit over leafy vegetables. Tegus require fresh water, and if their dish is large enough they may submerge, then curl up contentedly and soak for hours. They may also defecate in their water dish, so water quality must be closely monitored.

Useful Addresses and Literature

Bibliography

Auffenberg, Walter. *Behavioral Ecology of the Komodo Monitor.* Gainesville, Florida: University of Florida Press, 1981.

____. *Gray's Monitor Lizard.* Gainesville, Florida: University of Florida Press, 1988.

Avila-Pires,T.C.S. *Lizards of Brazilian Amazonia (Reptilia: Squamata).* Leiden: National Natural History Museum, 1995.

Bennett, Daniel. "A Review of Some Literature Concerning the Rough-Necked Monitor Lizard, *Varanus rudicollis.*" *Reptilian* (1)9, 1993.

____. "Dumeril's Monitor Lizard, *Varanus dumerilii.*" *Reptilian* (3)3, 1994.

____. "The Water Monitor, *Varanus salvator.*" *Reptilian* (3)8, 1995.

Boyer, Donal M. & W. E. Lamereaux. "Captive Reproduction and Husbandry of the Pygmy Mulga Monitor, *Varanus gilleni,* at the Dallas Zoo." Thurmont, Maryland. Proceedings of the 7th Annual Reptile Symposium on Captive Propagation and Husbandry, 1984.

Branch, Bill. *Bill Branch's Field Guide to the Snakes and Other Reptiles of Southern Africa.* Sanibel Island, Florida: Ralph Curtis Publishing, 1990.

Cogger, Harold G. *Reptiles and Amphibians of Australia.* Ithaca: Cornell/Comstock, 1992.

Eidenmuller, Berndt. "Successful Breeding of the Merten's Monitor Lizard, *Varanus mertensi.*" *The Vivarium* (7)2, 1995.

Hurt, C. "The Red Tegu." *Reptiles Magazine* (3)1, 1995.

Langerwerf, Bert. "Keeping and Breeding the Argentine Black and White Tegu, *Tupinambis teguixin.*" *The Vivarium* (7)3, 1995.

Linville, Paula. "Komodo Dragons and the National Zoo." *Reptiles Magazine* (3)8, 1995.

Sprackland, Robert G. *Giant Lizards.* Neptune City, New Jersey: TFH., 1992.

Walsh, Trooper, R. Rosscoe, G. Birchard. "Dragon Tales: The History, Husbandry and Breeding of Komodo Monitors at the National Zoological Park." *The Vivarium* (4)6, 1993.

Affinity Groups

Herpetoculture is no longer an obscure hobby. Hobbyists may be surprised to find how many others share their interests in keeping monitor, tegus, and related lizards. Detailed additional information can be as close as the closest fellow hobbyist. You can find other hobbyists through your local pet store, your local library, local university or community college, or "on-line" via a computer network such as Internet, Compuserve, Prodigy, and Herp-Net.

Another source of information is through herpetology groups. There are generalized groups of hobbyists in many large cities of the world, as well as professional societies such as the Society for the Study of Reptiles and Amphibians (SSAR). Tegus have no society of their own; the following are sources of information about monitors.

Varanid Information Exchange
8726D S. Sepulveda Blvd.
243
Los Angeles, CA 90045

Herpetologically Oriented Ecotours
Green Tracks
P.O. Box 9516
Berkeley, CA 94709
800-966-6539 (United States only)
or 510-526-1339 worldwide

Magazines
Reptile & Amphibian Magazine, RD3, Box 3709-A, Pottsville, PA 17901.

Reptiles Magazine, P.O. Box 6050, Mission Viejo, CA 92690-6050

The Vivarium: Available by membership in the American Federation of Herpetoculturists, P.O. Box 300067, Escondido, CA 92030-0067

The Reptilian Magazine, 22 Firs Close, Hazlemere, High Wycombe, Bucks HP15 7TF, England

Professional journals—available only to members of the societies or, occasionally, through used-book sellers.

Herp Review, and a more scholarly journal, *Journal of Herpetology,* available from the Society for the Study of Reptiles and Amphibians, Department of Zoology, Miami University, Oxford, OH 45056

Copeia (a technical journal) Business Office, Dept. of Zoology, Southern Illinois University, Carbondale, IL 62901-6501

Glossary

agonistic aggressive or defensive behavior

allopatric not occurring together but often in adjacent geographic areas

ambient temperature the temperature of the surrounding environment

anterior toward the front

anus the external opening of the cloaca; the vent

arboreal tree-dwelling

autotomize to use the ability to break easily or cast off (and usually regenerate) a part of the body, as in tail breakage in lizards

caudal pertaining to the tail

cloaca the common chamber into which digestive, urinary, and reproductive systems empty and that itself opens through the vent or anus

con... as used here, a prefix indicating "the same"; (congeneric refers to species in the same genus; conspecific indicates the same species)

deposition as used here, the laying of eggs

deposition site the spot chosen by the female to lay her eggs

dichromatic two color phases of the same species, often sex-linked

dimorphic a difference in form, build, or coloration in the same species; often sex-linked

diurnal active in the daytime

dorsal pertaining to the back; upper surface

dorsolateral pertaining to the upper sides

dorsum the upper surface

endemic confined to a specific region

estivation a period of warm weather inactivity; often triggered by excessive heat or drought

form an identifiable species or subspecies

fracture planes softer areas in the tail vertebrae that allow the tail to break easily if seized

genus a classification of a group of species having similar characteristics. The genus falls between the next broader designation of "family" and the next narrower designation of "species." *Genera* is the plural of *genus*. The generic name is always capitalized and italicized.

gravid the reptilian equivalent of mammalian pregnant

gular pertaining to the throat

heliothermic pertaining to a species that basks in the sun to thermoregulate

hemipenes the dual copulatory organs of male lizards and snakes

hemipenis the singular form of *hemipenes*

hibernaculum a temperature-controlled shelter occupied during the winter by a dormant lizard

hybrid offspring resulting from the breeding of two species

hydrate to restore body moisture by drinking or absorption

insular as used here, island-dwelling

intergrade offspring from the breeding of two subspecies

Jacobson's organ highly enervated sensory pits in the palate of snakes and lizards

juvenile a young or immature specimen

keel a ridge (along the center of a scale)

labial pertaining to the lips

lateral pertaining to the side

littoral seashore or seaside

melanism a profusion of black pigment, darker than normal

middorsal pertaining to the middle of the back

midventral pertaining to the center of the belly or abdomen

monotypic containing but one type

morphology study of the form and structure of animals and plants

ocelli outlined eye-shaped markings on the skin

oviparous reproducing by means of eggs that hatch after laying

poikilothermic a species with no internal body temperature regulation; "cold-blooded"

posterior toward the rear

race a subspecies

riparian riverine habitats

saurian any of a suborder of reptiles including the lizards

saxicolous rock-dwelling

species a group of similar creatures that produce viable young when breeding. The taxonomic designation narrower than *genus* and broader than *subspecies*

subcaudal beneath the tail

subspecies the subdivision of a species, a race that may differ slightly in color, size, scalation, or other criteria

SVL snout-vent length

sympatric occurring in the same range without interbreeding

taxonomy the science of classification of plants and animals

terrestrial land-dwelling

thermoregulate to regulate body temperature by choosing a warmer or cooler environment

tympanum the external eardrum

vent the external opening of the cloaca; the anus

venter the underside of a creature; the belly

ventral pertaining to the undersurface or belly

ventrolateral pertaining to the sides of the venter (belly)

Note: Other scientific definitions are contained in the following two volumes:

Peters, James A. *Dictionary of Herpetology.* New York: Hafner Publishing Co., 1964.

Wareham, David C. *The Reptile and Amphibian Keeper's Dictionary.* London: Blandford, 1993.

Index

Numbers in **boldface** type indicate color photos.